T0381461

ENDORSEMENTS

"I learned so much from Howes' work. I never imagined the history of Rome's army and their battle tactics could illuminate the rich meaning of Ephesians 6. This book will help you fight your spiritual battles and win."

John Duncan,
Pastor of Gateway Church, Ruidoso NM

"This is a fascinating book. I'd describe it as a history book overlayed on Scripture with inserts of tactical battle plans, which bring familiar Bible passages to life a new and inspiring way. The thorough explanations of Roman military life give meaning to multiple aspects of the New Testament, specifically the armor – I could see in my mind the legions of Roman soldiers, and I felt challenged to put on my armor. This book illuminates the promise that we've been given what we need to fight the battles of life."

Karis McCollum,
Assistant to the President,
KERYGMA VENTURES

This book brings alive the realities of ancient Roman warfare and effectively applies them to our spiritual warfare today. We often miss many of the implications of what God is telling us, because our world is so much different than the realities of the time. Upon reading this, your confidence in your Commander will be strengthened and so will your prayer life.

Micah Yoder, former missionary to Ecuador with Reach Beyond

Spiritual Warfare & the Armor of GOD

Conquering Adversity
Through the Power of God

MARTY HOWES

WESTBOW
PRESS®
A DIVISION OF THOMAS NELSON
& ZONDERVAN

WestBow Press books may be ordered through booksellers or by contacting:

WestBow Press
A Division of Thomas Nelson & Zondervan
1663 Liberty Drive
Bloomington, IN 47403
www.westbowpress.com
844-714-3454

Cover and Interior Image Credit: Dolores Chacon

Bible Citation: All scripture is taken from ESV unless otherwise noted.

ISBN: 979-8-3850-3661-5 (sc)
ISBN: 979-8-3850-3660-8 (e)

Library of Congress Control Number: 2024922494

Print information available on the last page.

WestBow Press rev. date: 01/25/2025

"HAVE I NOT COMMANDED YOU?
BE STRONG AND COURAGEOUS.
DO NOT BE FRIGHTENED, AND
DO NOT BE DISMAYED, FOR
THE LORD YOUR GOD IS WITH
YOU WHEREVER YOU GO."

JOS 1:9 ESV

CONTENTS

PROLOGUE

We have all seen or heard books and sermons about the Armor of God. Most have come from the place of good intent. Some have even been successful at delivering the original purpose of the message that the Apostle Paul was conveying to the believers in Ephesus. But not often do we see anyone share the historical context of this illustration, and apply it to the spiritual message that God has for us.

As it turns out, not all armor is created equal. And, as it is for understanding much of the Bible, context matters, particularly to realize the fullness of God's message.

There are many illustrations in the Bible: running a good race, the potter and the clay, sowing and reaping etc. They are helpful in making the wisdom of God more accessible to a wider audience of readers. That's why Jesus used parables to instruct God's wisdom. Few are as broadly applicable, and as richly beneficial, as grasping the reality of "spiritual warfare" and the "armor of God". That's because not everyone farms, or runs, or makes stuff out of clay. But everyone struggles with things in life. Everyone fights or struggles with something or someone.

Many business professionals study the military experience as a means to devise an advantage over the competition. They try to understand discipline, leadership and how to prioritize multiple layers of activity. The military community has made a profession out of how to perceive a struggle. How to make sense of it and, how to build reliable and repeatable modes of conduct within the struggle so that it can be overcome with certainty. This is not just a sword and sandal illustration of 'guy stuff.' It is for everyone, everywhere, who wants to live confidently in God's will. Every day. Joyously, productively, purposefully.

I've been studying the ancient history of western civilization since I was ten years old. It's Mr. Seleki's fault. He was my social studies teacher, and he was good. He brushed the surface of this genre in a way that was tangible to preteens. We had projects. My buddy and I made a cardboard model of ancient Babylon. I was hooked, and I never quit reading the genre. Especially the Romans. As an adult the similarities between the Roman republic and our own American republic added an interesting twist to an already life long passion. Then came Jesus, and I could only but surrender to Him. What profound delight I found, to realize that my understanding of ancient western civ history, all the research time, all the books, added context, texture and depth to the words of the Bible I was absorbing at a voracious rate.

There is always a back-story. God has preserved His word exactly as we need it. The human experience hasn't changed because human nature hasn't changed. As General Sir John Hackett observed in *Warfare In The Ancient World*, "One of the clearest conclusions emerging from a study of the distant past is that human nature, in all the time which we have record of it, has changed very little, if at all." We're all still born into the sin of the first Adam. That's why we need the Bible now as much as people needed it the day the books were written. What has changed are the cultures and languages of the human experience. Time has moved on. Linguistic nuances, cultural change and technological growth have obscured some of the details of what we read in the scriptures. They're still there, we just need to work harder to dig up the buried knowledge.

In this book, we will unlock the 'not so' secret information with which Paul knew his contemporary readers would conceptualize the illustration of the armor of God. We'll see how this adds greater depth and understanding to the message. We'll answer the questions: "What was military armor in the Roman world of Paul?" We'll consider "What was life like in the first century after Jesus' birth?" And, "What was warfare like in the times the Bible was written?" We can then apply that knowledge to the spiritual messages God has for us about "Spiritual Warfare and the Armor of God".

This could be transformative in how we view our everyday walk as believers. It could be instrumental in our success, in biblical terms, in living out God's will for us. It could lead to a better understanding of what we experience every day, and how we respond to those experiences. Most importantly, it may lead to a better understanding of our relationship with the Lord Jesus Christ and how our complete and utter dependency on Him is paramount to our peace, joy and contentment.

As a disclaimer, this book is not – a discourse on anything related to humanistic or new age interpretations of spiritual warfare via spiritualism or mysticism.

This book is – a window of understanding the Bible within the context of historical information now available to us. Then determining how this is most useful to our biblical worldview as Christ followers.

Often in church environments, it's customary to use 'shorthand' phrases to express oneself. We'll try to avoid such dialogue to instead be more specific and clear in our expressions of biblical application.

So let's look at how to better understand our daily life in Christ and how we are equipped to thrive.

All scripture is taken from ESV unless otherwise noted.

PART 1

Spiritual Warfare

CHAPTER 1

What is spiritual warfare ?

"Spiritual warfare... is something we're all born into because the human condition
is contrary to the perfection of God. ...recognize it for what it is
and strive purposefully toward the goals we hope to attain."   ~ Matthew Henry
Choose your side.

Grace
the perfection of God

Corruption
the human condition

"For I joyfully agree with the law of God
in the inner person, but I see a different
law in the parts of my body waging war
against the law of my mind, and making
me a prisoner of the law of sin..."

Romans 7:22-23.

1

The Root Cause

Romans chapter 7 is an almost humorous discourse about how Paul doesn't do what he wants to, and does what he doesn't want to. It's also a concise description of spiritual warfare.

The constant battle of right and wrong is something everyone experiences, whether Christ-follower or not, although we identify right and wrong by the perfection of God. He is perfect in honesty, judgment and compassion. While we are created in the image of God, we reflect an imperfect image of God's character because of the nature humanity has inherited from the rebellion of Adam and Eve. "Therefore, just as sin came into the world through one man, and death through sin, and so death spread to all men because all sinned" *Rom 5:12*.

These imperfections in our reflection of God are whats 'wrong' in the world. This immorality and misdeed is seen at minimum as an offense to God, and often as criminally punishable in the courts of our biblically based legal systems.

How a person deals with the struggle speaks to their morals, character and ethical values. The Apostle Pauls thinks it's particularly important for the Christian to pay careful attention. This issue affects every thought, how we process every experience, every response, every decision – every day. Yet how often do we consider this conflict even as it's happening? What is God seeing as He's watching?

Warfare itself goes back farther than we have records for. There is evidence of warfare in the rock art of our ancestors even before writing was introduced. People gathered, coordinated and sought ways to overpower their enemies. The methods of warfare evolved over time, and more efficient means of doing harm to one another were created.

Spiritual warfare goes back even farther. It was there in the garden of Eden. Even before that, it was introduced to God's creation the first time an angel rebelled against God. Once rebellion against God established itself in His creation, it propagated as fast as the children of Adam and Eve. It began to manifest itself in ways that we read about in stories like Cain and Abel, where Cain, as far as we can tell, introduced the first occurrence of violence into the world. Mankind began to struggle with spiritual warfare. As humanity has done for millennia, God's enemies have refined their onslaught against the kingdom of God so that now it's sometimes difficult to even recognize when we face a threat of spiritual warfare.

Spiritual warfare is your coworker wanting you to participate in a lie to your boss. "It's not a big deal. Should I just keep my mouth shut and go along? I don't want to be a pariah in my workplace." Spiritual warfare is your human nature compelling you to act unkindly to your spouse, or a stranger on the street, or in an office where you begrudgingly must do business. Spiritual warfare is the desire to be lazy about prioritizing the Lord in your life. It's the attempt to ignore the Holy Spirit when God says you're ready for action.

Spiritual warfare is every encounter that challenges your efforts to reflect the holiness of Christ. El Shaddai, the All Sufficient One, sees our worldly concerns, but He cares more about the people experiencing the concerns than the actual issues themselves. God is above these issues. He sees the end of the conflict and He is busy establishing the path of His people through the concerns of the world, towards the result that comfort is found amidst our struggles of worldly concern. "For the kingdom of God is not a matter of eating and drinking but of righteousness and peace and joy in the Holy Spirit." *Rom 14:17*

The Path Forward

The way we navigate these issues, our conduct in this spiritual warfare, has a lasting impact on the world around us and the kingdom of God. Don't think so? Well, that's why you're still reading about Job, and King David, and Hosea, and... Judas. "Look carefully then how you walk, not as unwise but as wise, making the best use of the time, because the days are evil. Therefore do not be foolish, but understand what the will of the Lord is." *Eph 5:15-17*

Paul says to the Corinthian believers, "For though we walk in the flesh, we are not waging war according to the flesh." *2 Cor 10:3* This word "WAR" Paul used is rooted in the idea of an active duty soldier, but has specific application: it refers to someone who is committed to spiritual truth and the action of contending against sin. A Roman soldier was committed to the actions required by his commander because of his devotion to his commander.

His commander didn't require of him in vain. The commander promised a return on the soldier's commitment with things the soldier could otherwise never hope to attain. That is, in the short term, all his worldly needs would be met. Better diet and health care than all but the wealthiest could afford. More importantly, the long term commitments of the commander were offers of security via retirement benefits and Roman citizenship. We see a similar relationship between the christian and the Lord God of Israel. He offers the believer what is otherwise unattainable, that is, grace to defer the penalty of our sin nature because Jesus paid it for us, and citizenship in the kingdom of God. Likewise in the short term, the care and guidance of a perfect Father.

The one element left in question with this parallel is: are believers as committed to El Shaddai, the All Sufficient One, as even a Roman soldier was to his commander? Where is that Christian who is, as Paul's idea of "waging war" suggests, on behalf of his redeemer, committed to spiritual truth and the action of contending against sin?

Spiritual warfare isn't something we participate in only after deciding to do some hard task for altruistic reasons, only then declaring ourselves a willful participant. No. It is something we're all born into because the human condition is contrary to the perfection of God. As Matthew Henry describes it "conflict between grace and corruption in the heart, between the law of God and the law of sin." So we have a choice. We can ignore the struggle and stumble through the process wishing for positive results, or we can seek to understand it, recognize it for what it is and strive purposefully toward the goals we hope to attain.

Paul says "Wretched man that I am! Who will deliver me from the body of this death?" *Rom 7:24*. That is, the physical body, born into sin that strives against the spiritual laws of God. Well, Paul immediately answers that for us too: "Thanks be to God through Jesus Christ our Lord…" The single and complete source of our success is found in Him.

Following are principles, truths and realities of the military experience, and what we can learn and apply to this reality of "spiritual warfare."

CHAPTER 2

COMMAND

"And there is nothing a Roman soldier enjoys more than the sight of his commanding officer eating the same bread as him or lying on a plain straw mattress, or lending a hand to dig a ditch or raise a palisade. What they admire in a leader is the willingness to share in danger and hardship, rather than the ability to win them honor and wealth"

Gaius Marius

The command structure of a military organization is the foundation by which everything else is built. As in many following examples, we'll use the Roman army organization of the early principate (1st century A.D.) because it was the ruling example contemporary to New Testament biblical authors. Rome began asserting authority with incursions into the Greek world in the early 2nd century B.C. and, nearly 3 centuries later, during Paul's time, was the master of the entire Mediterranean basin.

In the legions of Imperial Rome, there was certainly an effective structure of command from junior officers *Optio* (lieutenant) then *Centurio* (captain), to higher positions of *Tribunus militum* (colonel) and *Legatus legionis* (general) ultimately under command of the *Praetor* (major-general), under whom multiple legions were grouped as the overall Army Commander.

Most importantly was the commander-in-chief. From the time of Augustus Caesar onward, the emperor was the recognized commander of the entire Roman military machine. The Roman legionnaire swore an oath upon acceptance of his recruitment, the *sacramentum*, to the emperor. The emperor dictated the orders. He issued the equipment needed to accomplish those orders, distributed the necessities of life like food, drink and pay, ensured their training and provided for their future with retirement plans. The emperor created an environment wherein the legionary could be successful, and the most reliable way for the soldiers to meet with success was to be obedient.

Julius Caesar, though slightly earlier during the late Roman republic of the 1st century B.C., gives an example of the importance of this obedience in his book *The Gallic Wars*. During action at Gergovia in central France, after attempting to maneuver troops in the face of superior enemy forces, Caesar called a retreat. However many soldiers remembered previous victories and were hungry for another, and so the soldiers continued to advance, resulting in defeat. After eventually retrieving his army back to camp Caesar addressed his troops. "Much as I admire the heroism that you showed... I cannot too strongly condemn your bad discipline and your presumption in thinking that you know better than your commander-in-chief how to win a victory or foresee the result of an action. I want obedience and self restraint from my soldiers, just as much as courage in the face of danger." This is an articulate description of why obedience is important. The commander sees the big picture and is best positioned to know what to do next. The soldier, who isn't privy to all the details, must trust his commander and follow him. Also, the commander is ultimately responsible for success or failure. For his part when one finds themselves accountable for enterprises which include the action of others, it affects every decision and how one prioritizes the details. It's why a child who wants to play in the street, only caring about their immediate happiness, is told 'no' by the parent who is ultimately responsible that the child reaches adulthood in the safest way possible. This lack of responsibility is why the christian who doesn't see the future and all the details of life like God does, isn't so concerned about their decision to disobey the commandment of God.

To the Christ follower that's paying attention, this is compelling imagery for spiritual warfare, but let's be really, really clear about who is our commander.

Jehovah-Sabaoth

Going back a little farther, to the 15th century B.C., the nation of Israel just entered the promised land. NOW there's warfare to be had. Joshua, their leader, wondering how this surviving generation of desert wanderers can possibly capture one of the oldest fortified cities in human civilization, finds a place to be alone in sight of the city and consider his situation. "When Joshua was by Jericho, he lifted up his eyes and looked, and behold, a man was standing before him with his drawn sword in his hand. And Joshua went to him and said to him, 'Are you for us or for our adversaries?' And he said 'No; but I am the commander of the army of the Lord. Now I have come.' And Joshua fell on his face to the earth and worshiped and said to him, 'What does my Lord say to his servant?' And the commander of the Lord's army said to Joshua, 'Take off your sandals from your feet, for the place where you are standing is holy.' And Joshua did so." *Jos 5:13-15*.

That Joshua was not deterred from his worship of this individual makes it clear that this was none other than the Lord himself. An Old Testament appearance of the Christ. Now the Lord describes himself as the Captain of the host of the Lord; Jehovah-Sabaoth. Not that He is the leader of just the followers of Jehovah, but specifically *tsaba - the host* of a called out mass of individuals prepared for battle awaiting the movement into action. Joshua was the leader of potentially over 2 million people. Certainly this is a position of considerable power by any measure. Yet he, without hesitation, gave obeisance to his Captain and asked "what do you command your servant?" To better understand why this response was so quick, we need to look back to Joshua's first known experience leading God's people in battle.

Not long after leaving Egypt and crossing the Red Sea, Amalek came to fight the wandering mass of Israel in Rephidim, because most indigenous societies don't appreciate mass migrations of foreigners intruding on their land. Israel had a problem, but God had a plan. "And Moses said to Joshua, [Choose for us men, and go out and fight with Amalek. Tomorrow I will stand on the top of the hill with the staff of God in my hand.]" *Ex 17:9.* What must have Joshua thought about that? Moses would stand on a hill with a stick in his hand while Joshua and his chosen men went to great exertions to risk life and limb. Whether Joshua knew it or not, as long as the staff of God was held aloft, the Israelites prevailed. Moses, Aaron and Hur so believed the word of God that they found a way to keep the staff held high despite Moses' physical inability to do so, and Israel prevailed.

Now, as Joshua was standing there before Jericho with his Captain, the battle at Rephidim was decades ago, but "Then the Lord said to Moses, Write this as a memorial in a book and recite it in the ears of Joshua…" *Ex17:14.* God wanted Joshua to remember how He works and perhaps this memory is what motivated Joshua to respond as he did to the bizarre battle plan his Captain gave him for the siege of Jericho.

In the New Testament, Hebrews 2:10 describes Christ as the Captain of our salvation. "For it became him, for whom are all things, and by whom are all things, in bringing many sons unto glory, to make the captain of their salvation perfect through sufferings." Here we see Christ raising a group for whom He is their Captain. The chief leader. The author, inventor, architect and source of their eternal security. These people have a place in God's plans. Paul mentions this group of people five other times in the letter as *metochos - partaker,* and from these five instances we learn something about whom He's leading.

Heb 1:9, "You have loved righteousness and hated wickedness; therefore God, your God, has anointed you with the oil of gladness beyond your companions." Christ the Captain exists in a place of supremacy above the group of people who are all *partakers* of an anointing. This common anointing we have with Jesus is that of The Holy Spirit according to 1Jn 2:20.

Heb 3:1, "Therefore, holy brothers, you who share in a heavenly calling, consider Jesus, the apostle and high priest of our confession." The group has a heavenly calling. This calling was God's invitation into the new vocation of following Him, with Christ the Captain as the advocate of this calling.

Heb 3:14, "For we have come to share in Christ, if indeed we hold our original confidence firm to the end." The group shares in Christ, which according to Matthew Henry in his commentaries, refers to the Spirit, nature, graces and righteousness of Christ. This is conditionally dependent upon the individual holding to the original confidence originally assumed towards God. Presumably this is because once an attitude of mistrust develops, affections and resolutions become more self-centric, or at least rebellious to God.

Heb 6:4, "For it is impossible, in the case of those who have once been enlightened, who have tasted the heavenly gift, and have shared in the Holy Spirit, along with the common anointing of the Holy Spirit." While this statement is part of a dialogue on the dynamics of commitment, it also claims that the group has been enlightened (to godly wisdom) and tasted the heavenly gift (of salvation).

Heb 12:8, "If you are left without discipline, in which all have participated, then you are illegitimate children and not sons." The group experiences discipline as children of the heavenly Father.

This group is us, the church. The called out assembly (of believers) of God. More specifically this group is among the church. Paul is instructing on the experience of suffering, enduring hardship in 'The Way' of Christ. This group he is speaking about here are those people among the church that haven't wavered from the spiritual warfare into which they were called. These people, he says, follow Jesus the high priest into their own called priesthood of service to God.

This group is mentioned also in the letter to the Romans. "and if children, then heirs—heirs of God and fellow heirs with Christ, provided we suffer with him in order that we may also be glorified with him." *Rom 8:17.* Notice here the distinction between *kleronomos - one who shares a lot by inheritance,* and *sugkleronomos - one who has a common place in the inheritance with Christ,* so that one group has access to the inheritance and the other is further acknowledged by their engagement in spiritual warfare. The distinction is made by way of being exalted to a position of dignity together with Christ. The end result of this divergence is clarified by Paul to Timothy. "If we have died with him, we will also live with him; if we endure, we will also reign with him; if we deny him, he also will deny us; if we are faithless, he remains faithful." *2 Tim 2:11-12.* When one's old nature of rebellion dies

13

with a spiritual rebirth in Christ, our eternal security is guaranteed. This is made clear by Paul's additional statement about the divinely perfect faithfulness of Christ. However, within that group, those who display the fortitude of perseverance through spiritual warfare will also reign with Him. This is in reference to God's future plans after His enemies are conclusively denied any further negative impact in the world.

Paul adds that it is possible to forego participation in spiritual warfare. One might accept the deceptions of God's enemies, ignore opportunities to uphold the principles of biblical truth and reject any guidance offered by God through the Holy Spirit. In doing so one would be refusing to follow the path and the priesthood of service God has prepared for them. This denial will be equally met by the Lord denying this person any distinction in His future plans. Amazingly though, despite any such faithless refusal to participate, God will remain true to His commitment of care for His people.

So then, in the Old Testament we see the Messiah leading a host armed for war. In the New Testament we see Him leading a church armed with something more unexpected and potent: salvation.

Three Aspects of Salvation

In his study on Paul's letter to the Roman church, Pastor (retired) Ken Hornock of Midvalley Bible Church in Utah, draws on wisdom of the pillars of church history to articulate with contemporary clarity, the three aspects of salvation in Christ: "1) justification from past sin, 2) transformation away from the present power of sin, 3) glorification from the presence of future sin."

First, Jesus takes us from a place of separation from God, and places us in a condition wherewith we can live in relationship with the Trinity of God. "And you, who once were alienated and hostile in your mind, doing evil deeds, he has now reconciled in his body of flesh by his death, in order to present you holy and blameless and above reproach before him" *Col 1:21,22.* According to Millard J. Erickson in *Christian Theology* this is the beginning of salvation. The conversion experience which according to Erickson is "the response of the human being to God's offer of salvation."

Then God remakes us into a creation suitable for work in the kingdom of God. It's the process which Erickson calls, 'the continuation of salvation.' "WE MUST have an unconditional readiness to change in order to be transformed in Christ," said Dietrich von Hildebrand, the outspoken critic of Naziism who escaped to the USA while being hunted down by the Gestapo. Paul encouraged the christians in Rome: "Do not be conformed to this world, but be transformed by the renewal of your mind, that by testing you may discern what is the will of God, what is good and acceptable and perfect." *Rom 12:1*-2. This means that by the transformation process, we can discover conclusively what God's will is for us. To know what is our priesthood, what is the path down which God wants to direct us. Erickson calls it, "the Holy Spirit's applying to the life of the believer, the work done by Jesus Christ." We know that it's the work of the Holy Spirit that must do the transforming, because the mind of our human nature inherited from Adam wants to conform to this world. This deviation of interests between our mind and the Holy Spirit is one of the reasons we experience spiritual warfare.

Finally, God maps out our very best future with Him. The final aspect of our salvation in Christ, our glorification, is what Erickson calls, the "completion of salvation," and he further explains that whether in death or through prophetic events, "the judgment will be the final declaration of the justified status of the believer. Paul excitedly says of this, "Behold! I tell you a mystery. We shall not all sleep, but we shall all be changed, in a moment, in the twinkling of an eye, at the last trumpet.

For the trumpet will sound, and the dead will be raised imperishable, and we shall be changed." *1 Cor 15:52-53.* Instantaneously our body and spirit will be changed into something imperishable and incorruptible of which Paul further says "the Lord Jesus Christ, who will transform our lowly body to be like his glorious body, by the power that enables him even to subject all things to himself. *Phil 3:20-21.* Yes, a glorious body like that which Jesus Christ had taken upon His ascension to heaven, will be the final development of the initial 'call on the name of the Lord' for the redemption of our hopeless condition without God.

With that, perhaps, it's easier to comprehend how our Lord the Christ is our Captain *archegos – chief leader, captain, prince* in spiritual warfare. He takes us in. He is the alpha and omega of our worldly existence. He conclusively affords our future well-being.

Following the Commander

As Caesar required obedience, so does the Lord our Captain and often for the same reasons. We can't possibly know better than our Captain how to achieve victory or foresee the result of any action we might take. To learn how God sees this, let's look at King Saul, God's chosen leader of the nation of Israel. God remembered how Amalek opposed Israel when they came up out of Egypt. So they were considered a threat to Israel's well being in the promised land. Samuel instructed Saul to fight the Amalekites and completely remove their presence from Israel. (To the Kenites who lived among the Amalekites,

17

they were instructed to evacuate the area because they showed kindness to Israel.) "But Saul and the people spared Agog and the best of the sheep and of the oxen and of the fattened calves and lambs, and all that was good, and would not utterly destroy them. All that was despised and worthless they devoted to destruction." *1 Sam 15:9*. What follows is one of those cringe-worthy moments in scripture. When Samuel comes to meet Saul,

The king greets him saying "God bless you, I have performed the commands of God"

Samuel responds, "then what's with all the sheep and oxen I hear? Why did you not obey the voice of the Lord?"

"But I did. I went on the mission God sent me. I beat and brought back king Agog and destroyed the Amalekites. But the people took the spoils of sheep and oxen to sacrifice to God."

"And Samuel said, Has the Lord as great delight in burnt offerings and sacrifices, as in obeying the voice of the Lord? Behold, to obey is better than sacrifice and to listen than the fat of rams." *1 Sam 15:22*.

As Caesar explained why it's important to obey in a practical sense, Samuel explains additionally that God likes it when we obey. It's just better. Better than taking the best cow - the best of your prized possessions, and sacrificing it to God. To listen, *Qashab - the give heed to*, is better than the pleasure derived from tasting the best part of the animal. That we would defer our desire and give heed to the word of God into obedience of His will, is the most pleasing thing to God. More pleasing than anything else we might do for God. YHWH had such desire that we obey Him, that He sent Jesus to the cross for us so that we might hear and recognize His voice. So we can follow Him, our Captain.

To understand or not, why God has us do things, is not the point. Many people feel like they need to know why, but God told Isaiah: "For my thoughts are not your thoughts, nor are your ways my ways," says the Lord. "For as the heavens are higher than the earth, so are my ways higher than your ways, and my thoughts than your thoughts." *Isa 55:8-9.* To the son of Adam living by the impulses of human nature, this might be a stumbling block. But to the child of God, raised to walk in newness of life, this is a source of great peace and security.

Something else we see of the Roman commander is that he was the central source of cohesion and confidence of the army. Where he was on the battlefield, there was the focused point of strength. Often when an area of the battlefield became desperate, the commander would go there, his presence inspiring the men to greater efforts and ultimate victory. So when the legionary commander Labienus was leading a smaller unit detached from Caesar's forces, he inspired his men thus: "Fight as bravely under me as you often have under the commander-in-chief; imagine that he is here, watching the battle in person." Labienus exhorts his soldiers; "Imagine." "Imagine!" Though Caesar was not there with them, he would quickly find out how they represented themselves and Caesar, in the coming engagement.

How limited are we to see beyond our immediate experience. And how limitless is God. "God is our refuge and strength, a very present help in trouble." *Ps 46:1.*

The commander we serve isn't just someone from whom we must seek inspiration while he's watching us. When we find ourselves in trouble, that is, when we are stuck in a spiritual battle, God is not only present but a very present help; *Matsa* - He *exists in our present company in complete sufficiency* to address whatever struggle assails us. By this the Lord becomes our foundation of strength to resist and conquer the challenge. By His sufficiency He also becomes our refuge *machseh*. Even in the midst of the struggle, if we can 'imagine' how perfectly God is present, His sufficiency is a place of rest in the struggle. But *machceh* also implies hope. In His sufficiency we can have the confident expectation of success, and of our future well-being. This very trait of God sets Him apart from all other gods. Even after the grace of remission of sin and the promise of living in His eternal presence, He wants to be 'very present' with His people, even while we still possess a nature completely contrary to Him.

The Roman commander watches the battlefield and moves to the struggling areas to inspire and take control. We know our Captain sees every part of every spiritual battle everywhere, because He is everywhere all the time. Even still, since Jesus' ascension to heaven, God accords every born-again believer with His Holy Spirit the moment His grace is applied. The Holy Spirit of God physically indwells His people. The commander is personally attentive to every person that knows spiritual warfare is coming to them, or who finds themselves in the midst of a struggle, or who is dealing with after-effects of a difficult struggle.

On the battlefield of the 1st century A.D., control by

the commander was maintained by various means. G.H. Donaldson, in *Signaling Communications and the Roman Imperial Army*, says "the Romans' use of both acoustical and visual signals to control units in combat is well attested." The Roman historian Vegetius elaborates in *De Re Militari*, "The trumpet sounds the charge and the retreat. The cornets are used only to regulate the motions of the colors…" Communication was challenging and the Romans utilized equipment to make the best of a difficult situation. They also used messengers running back and forth between the commander and the junior officers. Sometimes, the commander, as we've seen, just had to go there himself. Having the spirit of God with us, Jehovah-Shammah - God our companion will never lose command and control. There is no confusion about what we see and hear. No need for a go-between messenger. God tore open the veil between the the sanctuary of His presence and the outside world, and made obsolete the temple-centric worship of life under the law of Moses. So now it's just us and God, our Commander. God speaks to us as He's inclined to do, and we can come to Him whenever we need or want to.

We have seen the nature of a soldier's relationship with his captain. The soldier depends on his captain for life's sustenance and provisions for success, seeks his council for the present decisions and coming events, trusts his future to his captain, seeks his captain's approval, doesn't always understand his captain's wisdom (and accepts that) and most importantly realizes his captain's authority over him. Is that a description of our daily walk with God? Do we trust our Captain with our physical well being? Do we seek His council with money matters or decisions at work? Seek His approval in how we respond to people we share the road with while driving? Seek Him regarding our short term plans and long term future security? Trust His guidance regardless of our understanding?

Do we recognize Christ our Captain as the great leader described by Marius? Jesus ate the same bread as those He leads and participates in their life and work. More importantly Jesus experienced the hardships of life common to His followers and assumed danger on their behalf even to the point of suffering and death. Jesus Christ perfectly exemplified the commander of the famous Roman general's description.

LOGISTICS

"An army marches on its stomach"

Frederick the Great.

Practical Needs

The ancient Greek historian Herodotus, said Cambyses the Persian king "lost his wits completely" for embarking in anger on a military campaign without having made any logistical plans. His army attempting every available option, only to resort to cannibalism, returned home with great loss having accomplished nothing.

Within the Roman legions, the commander, with the help of the state, provided food, water, pay, construction tools, combat equipment, camp gear and all other necessary equipment. It has been estimated that a Roman army of 19,200 fighting men consumed over 68 tons of food per day plus "a staggering amount of water and firewood," *Brett Devereaux Total Generalship - Collections 2022.* According to Dr. Marcus Junkelmann the renowned experimental archaeologist and reenactor, the marching Roman soldier carried up to 120 lbs. With 80% of the marching kit being equipment and personal items, the remaining 20% food and only a small steel canteen or skin with water.

This marching kit is something that Jesus Christ spoke about to His disciples when He referred to the Roman Lex Angareia. A set of laws designed to aid in imperial logistics. The laws stated that within a Roman governed province, according to Jonathan Roth *Logistics of the Roman Army at War (264BC - 235 AD),* a Roman military officer can 'borrow for one mile' a local civilian to carry his equipment. Jesus, in *Mt 5:41,* said to carry this 100+lb pack an extra mile to offer an unexpected act of kindness, and also possibly, to peacefully undermine the small act of tyranny, thereby demonstrating that the peace of God is greater than Rome's temporal power.

For the common soldier, whether in garrison or on campaign, he gets up every day with a job to do. His understanding was that be it a day of marching, fighting, training or building, all aspects of the required tasks would be provided for. He just had to do the work.

For those who know God as Jehovah-Jireh, they know He "satisfies the longing soul, and the hungry soul He fills with good things." *Ps 107:8*. There are many places in the Bible that speak to the provision of God in diverse ways, and Jesus Himself provides insight into how the law of God works in our lives. "Therefore do not be anxious, saying, 'What shall we eat?' Or 'What shall we drink?' Or 'What shall we wear?' For the gentiles seek after these things, and your heavenly Father knows that you need them all. But seek first the kingdom of God and His righteousness, and all these things will be added to you." *Mt 6:31-33*. He is instructing a life in which the Christian really doesn't need to spend time and emotional energy on concerns of this world, and because of that there is a supernaturally engendered freedom to occupy oneself instead with the concerns of God's kingdom.

Like the Roman soldier's oath to his commander, this requires a subordination of self to God. As Timothy Keller teaches: "If you want Jesus with you, you have to give up the right to self-determination." To the son of Adam this is a tough pill to swallow. To the person living under the laws of the modern man - humanistic, self worshiping and inexperienced to the goodness of God, this is impossible. To the believer in God that never followed the advice of the psalmist "Oh taste and see that the Lord is good! Blessed is the man who takes refuge in Him." *Ps 34:8,* this is still difficult to comprehend. Do you identify with one of these descriptions? Now you might be tempted to put this book down and walk away. After all, "the gate is narrow and the way is hard that leads to life, and those who find it are few". *Mt 7:14*

But consider the juxtaposition of Jesus mentioning gentiles in this matter in *Mt 6:32*. They are not godless people, but they are Jehovah-less people. Matthew Henry says of them "They fear and worship their idols, but know not how to trust them for deliverance and supply, and therefore are themselves full of care..." In the modern day, christian and non-believer alike still have idols. And they're the same old idols. So don't be like the 1st century A.D. gentiles.

The root of the issue is 'what we are seeking.' If the Roman soldier is out seeking his own well-being then he is not working as instructed for the well being of the empire. The only reason he would derelict himself of his duties at such great risk of physical punishment to himself, is thinking he could meet his own needs better than his commander could provide for him.

Timothy Keller in *"Rediscovering Jonah: The Secret of God's Mercy"* says this: "If you want to understand your own behavior, you must understand that all sin against God is grounded in a refusal to believe that God is more dedicated to our good, and more aware of what that is, than we are. We distrust God because we assume he is not truly for us, that if we give him complete control we will be miserable. Adam and Eve did not say, 'Let's be evil. Let's ruin our own lives and everyone else's too!' Rather they thought, 'We just want to be happy. But His commands don't look like they'll give us the things we need to thrive. We'll have to take things into our own hands—we can't trust him.'" In hindsight this sounds like lunacy but yet, modern believers do it all the time.

When Jesus said 'seek first the kingdom of God', He meant - to consider the will of God (His plan for you) as the highest priority, and execute it by faith to the service of the kingdom of God. Matthew Henry says this "is the sum and substance of our whole duty."

In doing so the creator of the universe has obligated Himself to you. Nothing of our own doing, God made this commitment to us. When we consume ourselves with things that are important to God, He'll care for what's important for us. The apostle Paul even provides some insight to why God would do that. "And God is able to make all grace abound to you, so that having all sufficiency in all things at all times, you may abound in every good work." *2 Cor 9:8*. God actually guarantees that in seeking first the kingdom of God, His grace will *abound* to you: *to cause super-abundance, to exceed, to have excess,* so that you are cared for enough to be free to concern yourself solely with the 'good works' that God requires of you.

Undoubtedly there is some confusion that builds around how this works, and for a couple of reasons.

Divine Economics

First - our worldly values are hard to reconcile with God's values, "send me money because God wants me to have a private jet!" Or more likely, "I'll just let society raise my kids because that will allow me to work more, so I can provide more material comfort for my family." In this regard, expecting God to be an accomplice in our selfishness to satiate ourselves with the cares of the world is, well, heresy. That message of justified materialism is not in the Bible. Following that path will lead to disillusionment in a misperceived Christ-centered worldview, and a disconnect between the believer and God's great plans.

It must be asked then, what will actually be provided? This second point is nothing short of miraculous in that it actually defies the laws of physics and our instincts of self preservation. God's economy is not our economy. Here is our worldly reality: if we work enough or are smart enough, we can earn enough, to collect enough material comfort to even create our own peace.

God has a better plan. "For who has known the mind of the Lord? Or who has become His counselor?" *Rom 11:34*. What then, are the kingdom of God laws of provision?

It's a bold move to trust God with this. Can I be content with God's provision? Can I be happy living in the fullness of God's plan when I don't even know what it is?

Consider Jesus feeding the multitude of people who had come to hear Him speak. It's recorded that there were five thousand men, plus the women and children. To calculate rough logistical needs to feed the group we can start by just using the known figure of 5,000. Philip said "200 denarii worth of bread would not be enough for each of them to get a little" *Jn 6:7*. Now one denarii according to Jesus was a day's wage, which it was for a

Roman soldier, not necessarily for everyone. The buying power of money fluctuated then as it does today but 1 denarii would buy enough grain to make roughly 7 loaves of bread depending on the recipe. 200 denarii would buy 1,400 loaves. In the disciples mind, somehow there needed to have been enough work to receive earnings (or donations) of at least 300 denarii for everyone to eat a half loaf of bread. That's 300 days wages from a good paying job! But that would have only fed the 5,000 men. Imagine the complete breakdown of logistics in the mind of the disciples.

Then Jesus applied kingdom of God economics. He fed the 5,000 and didn't need 300 days wages, He only needed one boy to make himself available to God. *Jn 6:8.* How valuable were those 5 barley loaves and 2 fish in the midst of a hungry crowd of 5,000 people? That boy could have made a lot of money that day by selling his fish and bread, and been proud of himself. Instead, "seek first the kingdom of God," the boy gave all that he had to Jesus. He still ate and was filled but also saw Jesus feed the entire crowd with his little basket of food. "And all these things will be added to you." By giving all he had to Jesus, the boy showed by his actions that he believed Jesus, trusted Jesus, and would rather have Jesus with him than any profits he might have realized by selling his food at inflated prices to the hungry crowd. As if being part of a miracle of God wasn't enough, there was left over, a net increase from his original 5 loaves, to 12 baskets full of bread. Whether the disciples kept it for further distribution or it was returned to the boy, this shows a principle that we'll see become a common pattern in the

Bible. That if we expect God to increase or improve our situation, we must give Him what we have. Not store it away like 'responsible disciples' or consume it ourselves because 'we have to take care of ourselves so we can take care of others.' Note: this doesn't change a thing about God's commission to Adam, and his descendants, to work. *See Gen 3:17.* Additionally about your work, applying the kingdom principle above, if you want God's blessing over your work efforts, you must give the heart of your work efforts to Him. Do we show up to work every day because we're working towards the next new car or boat or...? Or do we show up as an ambassador for Christ serving God in the workplace?

And so goes the principle, in keeping with the parable examples from God. Paul speaks of it to the Corinthian church, "he who sows sparingly will also reap sparingly, and he who sows bountifully will also reap bountifully." *2 Cor 9:6.* Because of this dynamic, His blessings often (not necessarily always, because He won't just be predictable for our sakes) come in kind to what we're willing to give him. For example, I know a woman who considered that her career was her ministry and priesthood. She found the best way to experience God's blessing over her job was to subordinate the very heart of her desire to succeed in her career, to the expectations of God. This meant following His guidance wherever He sent her, enjoying all the good and enduring all the difficult experiences awaiting her while bearing the conduct that allows the Lord to impact that workplace. She then found the contentment of seeing the supernatural empowerment of God giving her the wisdom and patience to make decisions and interact with coworkers as a faithful Christ follower. As in the way Jesus chose to feed the 5000 was through the commitment of one boy's gift of food, so this woman's workplace is blessed by her commitment to Godly workplace practices.

This pattern is seen in the Old Testament too. The widow visited by the prophet Elijah in *1 Ki 17:6-16* learned about God's economy. The widow was, presumably a gentile, living in Sidon. A city so strong as to never have been subdued by the tribe of Asher, whose lot Sidon was located within. God instructed Elijah to go there because "a widow would sustain him". Upon arrival he found the widow gathering sticks to cook with. The land was experiencing drought and famine and she had just about no food, cooking oil or water left. Elijah didn't know that about her and probably didn't expect it because God said she would sustain him. When Elijah bade her bring him some bread, she replied, "As the Lord your God lives, I have nothing baked, and only a handful of flour in a jar and a little oil in a jug. And now I am gathering a couple of sticks that I may go in and prepare it for myself and my son, that we may eat it and die." In her gentile mind, the Lord was Elijah's god, *Elohim - a supreme god over all the other gods.* None of whom could be relied upon in time of need.

Elijah instructs her "Do not fear," and saying "first make me a little cake and bring it to me, and afterward make something for yourself and your son. For thus says the Lord, the God of Israel, The jar of flour shall not be spent, and the jug of oil shall not be empty, until that day the Lord sends rain upon the earth." In keeping with the pattern we're seeing, God wants to bless the woman with providing her food, but first requires her by faith to give of what little food she yet has. Also in keeping with the pattern, faith is rewarded in ways we can't imagine.

Now Elijah is teaching the widow about God's economy. Even though the little gods people worship can't be depended upon, the God of Israel, Jehovah the creator of the laws of physics gives His attention to this poor, hungry widow. 'Don't be afraid for your well being, because if you seek first the kingdom of God, by tending to someone else's well being before your own, then not only will He tend to your immediate needs but also provide for your future.' By her action, she showed faith in God's commitment to her, and as time went on realized "she and her household ate for many days. The jar of flour was not spent, neither did the jug of oil become empty, according to the word of the Lord spoken by Elijah." As the biblical pattern goes, it was the very thing she gave to God, that was supernaturally multiplied for her.

Part of living in God's economy is understanding His value system. How often have we walked through the halls of a church building or some other non-profit organization, and seen the names of wealthy people listed in order of how much they donated? Many see that and wish they had enough to give that much too. Those people haven't grasped God's value system. "Jesus looked up and saw the rich putting their gifts into the offering box, and He saw a poor widow put in two small copper coins. And He said, Truly, I tell you, this poor widow has put in more than all of them. For they have contributed out of their abundance, but she out of her poverty put in all that she had to live on." *Lk 7:1-4.* Normally greater quantity equals greater value, but God values something more than simple physics. To say that God owns every beast of the forest and the cattle on a thousand hills is a gross understatement. But what does Ps 50:7-15 mean?

"Hear, O my people, and I will speak; O Israel, I will testify against you. I am God, your God. Not for your sacrifices do I rebuke you; your burnt offerings are continually before me." God had a problem with His people. Not because of their sacrifices: God was receiving an abundance of their offering which they were giving in accordance to the law.

"I will not accept a bull from your house or goats from your folds. For every beast of the forest is mine, the cattle on a thousand hills. I know all the birds of the hills, and all that moves in the field is mine. If I were hungry, I would not tell you, for the world and its fullness are mine. Do I eat the flesh of bulls or drink the blood of goats?" God says, 'I don't even want your animals, I own all the animals anyway. If I was hungry I wouldn't even tell you. Do you think I need your sacrifices for my own sustenance? Why are you even bothering to make the sacrifice if it's just because you feel obligated to keep the law?' "Offer to God a sacrifice of thanksgiving, and perform your vows to the Most High, and call upon me in the day of trouble; I will deliver you, and you shall glorify me." What's important to God is that we willingly call on Him because we seek His help, and that we make sacrifices to God not out of legal obligation, but as a thanksgiving because we recognize who He is for us and what He means to us. Then is He glorified through us.

Although as New Testament believers we don't need to make animal sacrifices, the apostle Paul, who knew as well as anyone about sacrifice requirements, gives us a new standard: "I appeal to you therefore, brothers, by the mercies of God, to present your bodies as a living sacrifice, holy and acceptable to God, which is your spiritual worship." *Ro 12:1.* All God wants is us, without reservation. God values people more than anything.

The thing about God's economy that's often misunderstood, because we tend to apply our limited realities to God, is that "seeking first the kingdom of God" is no guarantee of wealth or poverty. It IS a guarantee that you can be right where God wants you, that you'll have exactly what you need for the work/priesthood/ministry/daily life that God has ordained for you from the beginning – if you're willing to do it. And in that guarantee, He will care for you as if you were the only person in His world, offering you the joy and peace of the Holy Spirit that exists only in the kingdom of God.

Eventually this raises questions for the modern believer. Based on the economy in which you live, what god do you worship? How committed are you to "seek first the kingdom of God?" As it turns out, Jehovah-Sabaoth, the commander of the army, is also Jehovah-Jireh, the great provider. Success in spiritual warfare is largely dependent on the Christ-follower's ability and willingness to recognize that and act upon it.

CHAPTER 4

LEADERSHIP

The Roman soldier, aside from offering willingness to be dependent upon his commander, committed to go wherever the commander required of him. Legionnaires from Italy garrisoned the northern border of England. Legionnaires from France built bath houses in Africa. And legionnaires from Spain quelled a revolt in Palestine. Julius Caesar led several legions back and forth across western Europe for eight years forging circumstances that affect western civilization even today.

In 31 BC, Octavian (Caesar Augustus of biblical reference) ordered his troops to board a naval armada and, due to the difference in the enemy ships, Preston Chesser states "the battle progressed more as a land battle than a standard sea battle" *Ohio State University eHistory,* with Octavian's soldiers boarding and burning the enemy ships. The ensuing battle of Actium was the decisive victory over the forces of Marc Antony and Cleopatra.

In 69 AD, the commander Vespasian, after fighting the revolt in Judea for two years, suddenly ordered his men to march north through Turkey, then across eastern

Europe and on to Rome in an effort to conclude the civil war and become emperor, Michael Grant *The Twelve Caesars*. He founded a new dynasty.

In 74 AD, Flavius Silva the governor of the province of Syria led the venerated 10th legion to siege the Jewish citadel of Masada. They were then ordered to build a dirt ramp 450' high to access the fortress walls. This led to the conclusion of the Jewish revolt. Josephus *The Wars of the Jews*.

For the life of a Roman soldier, one never knew when a sudden order would come to march across a continent or embark on some hitherto unimaginable undertaking. When one set his mind on joining the legion, the course of his life became a mystery.

Imagine the foolishness of a Roman soldier waking up one morning and going about his daily business with complete indifference to the goals of his commander. "The heart of man plans his way, but the Lord establishes his steps." *Prov 16:9*. Similar to life in the legion, King Solomon expects people of God will set their hearts to seek first the kingdom of God, and as the Roman soldier understands the guarantee of his commanders support upon the commission of his obedience to orders, so Solomon explains how God supports His people.

Traveling God's Path

It starts with the heart of man planning- *Chashab (khaw-shab')- thinking, creating an idea, Zodhiates lexical aids*. When a Christ follower contrives in their mind to imagine what it would be like to live a life focused on the will of God, this can't stay hidden from God. As the song says "the Lord of Hosts is with us, the God of Jacob is our refuge. Selah." *Ps 46.* It is upon these conditions that God builds His work in us. To the willing heart and open mind the Holy Spirit *directs,* as some versions translate the proverb. It's easy to imagine an angelic hand grabbing us by the ankle and setting our foot where God wants it as He is directing our steps, but there is more to it than that.

God establishes (directs) our steps – *Kun- to set up, build, make ready, direct, be formed to aim, to attend to…* The main idea is to bring something into incontrovertible existence. This process passes through five phases according to *Zodhiates lexical aids.* And the phases are as follows:

1. Formation – God created a plan for us. We can embrace it or not, but He conceived this plan. It's the initial proposal, the development of the project. It's that we would be "His workmanship, created in Christ Jesus for good works, which God prepared beforehand, that we should walk in them." *Eph 2:10*. The 'good works' are the priesthood He is directing our steps towards. There is no telling how long, or the extent He has planned beforehand, so that we should live out His plan. Paul says we are born for this. The rebellious spirit of a person might read, 'we're born for a life of servitude? No way, not me.' The person walking in newness of life in Christ will read, 'I get to take part in the big plans of God? The creator of the universe has planned ahead to prepare a path for me. How awesome is that!?' The good works are likely to trigger spiritual warfare. Too often this leads to disillusionment, but as we'll see, this is also part of God's established path.

2. Preparation – the actual steps taken to prepare for a future event, like preparing the meal for a dinner event, or planning a military campaign in the buildup for a war. There is a lot of scripture that alludes to this dynamic without discussing it. But let's. The prophet Isaiah uses the illustration that "we are the clay and You are the potter, we are all the work of Your hand." *Isa 64:8*. The allusion is that the potter will not use the vessel until the time passes when he finished the work.

The use of the vessel requires the preparation of the vessel. Jesus explains of the shepherd and sheep: "When he has brought out all his own, he goes before them, and the sheep follow him, for they know his voice." *Jn 10:4.* The shepherd goes before them. They don't go out until the shepherd calls them. But perhaps there's conscientious sheep that are eager to be useful and have their wool sheared or are just ready to get the party going and get out to green pasture, sunshine and water. Can you imagine overzealous sheep wandering aimlessly not knowing where to find what they're looking for, or worse yet, wandering into a pack of wolves? Yet we know people just like that. The allusion here is that the shepherd takes time to prepare the way, finding good pasture and making the way safe. Then it's time for the sheep to follow the shepherd's calling. Isaiah in his prayer says: "From of old no one has heard or perceived by the ear, no eye has seen a God besides you, who acts for those who wait on Him" *Isa 64:4.* This 'waiting' on God's preparation can be difficult. We can't see Him working. We don't even know when He is, or if He is working. There now, is a source of real spiritual warfare; to wait on God or to take matters into our own hands. It just feels good to be doing something. Like the sheep analogy that often leads directly to a pack of wolves. The reason that is so likely and common, is because the enemies of God aren't sleeping. They are actively seeking weakness in God's kingdom, and those believers who aren't walking the path God has for them are vulnerable. Better to obey and wait on God's preparations. There is no other plan that guarantees positive results in spiritual warfare.

3. Creating - The soldier receives his orders. He doesn't hesitate. He knows the full weight of the authority of his commander is behind him. He goes out to perform his duties. For the Christian, the time has come to do the thing. The sheep have been called out to follow their shepherd. The clay vessel is sent to be used by whomever the potter has given it. The heavens are spoken into existence. The work of the believer has been launched. The book is being written, the workplace is seeing the fruits of the Spirit. The priesthood is being built/created/established.

In the book of Acts, we see things starting to come together for the apostles. They waited in the upper room. Jesus said things to them which seemed unbelievable at the time, but now the Holy Spirit had come and was teaching God's wisdom. Jesus made all needed preparations before His ascension and the time has come for the apostles to do the work that was planned for them. Paul explains what the apostles were experiencing. With the new covenant through Christ, it is now God's plan to make known to all the world, the wisdom of God, through the church. This is something God had planned from the beginning, that He accomplished through Christ in the fullness of time.

And because of that work of Christ, and our relationship with Him, we have access directly to God, through the Holy Spirit, to discover the riches of God's wisdom. *Eph 3:10-12 author's paraphrase.* This is our point of contact with God directing our paths. We can't fathom the plans He has created. We don't see the preparations He makes. But we know when He is calling us to something. Seeing the way Paul describes this, it's easy to envision the calling could be anything anywhere. Is the call to parenthood your ministry? Is your work, your ministry? Has He called you to some unexpected ministry? Is your priesthood a profession where God wants you to be His ambassador? In Acts chapter 5 we see the apostles coming to understand the completeness to which God has called them to build His kingdom. It's always like that. God's desire is that we are all in, 100%, no reservations. That was the issue with Ananias and Sapphira *Acts 5:1-4*. As we saw earlier, it's not that God has any need of our things. Our conduct in relation to materialism God considers, is a reflection of our heart toward Him. Ananias and Sapphira kept some of the proceeds of their land sale not because they needed the money, it was because they weren't fully committed to serving God. Later in Acts 5, Peter and the gang are arrested for preaching Jesus. When God mysteriously releases them, they're brought before the council and the following conversation shows the extent of their new found wisdom and vision of their work in Christ, which they had experienced since Pentecost.

The high priest addresses the apostles, "We strictly charged you not to teach in this name, yet here you have filled Jerusalem with your teaching, and you intend to bring this man's blood upon us."

Peter responds, "We must obey God rather than men. The God of our fathers raised Jesus, who you killed by hanging him on a tree. God exalted him at his right hand as Leader and Savior, to give repentance to Israel and forgiveness of sins. And we are witnesses to these things, and so is the Holy Spirit whom God has given to those who obey him." *Acts 5:28-32*

Given the gravity of the situation, the risk of personal injury and the reputation that will come from this response, it shows of the apostles, a strong commitment to a clear vision of the work God called them to. Christian, regardless of what the future holds, you have your contact point with God directing your path. Do you have a vision for it? Are you following? Are you all in?

4. Preservation – Traveling through Europe, one hears and sees the Roman Empire everywhere. There are no less than 24 languages and dialects derived from the Roman world. Aside from German and English, everywhere you go, you'll hear a language that's the legacy of the Roman Empire. And it's hard to go anywhere in Europe, North Africa or the Middle East without seeing structural remains of the empire. Aqueducts, amphitheaters and even entire towns. The work of the Roman soldier lives on even today. It wasn't all conquest. It was making trade routes safe. Creating safe spaces to live. Building – lots of building. Providing clean water and establishing

good hygiene. There are very few names of soldiers preserved, but their work endures. Twenty five times the word *Kun* is used to refer to the establishment of a dynasty, giving emphasis on the lasting nature of the line of rulers most notably in a reference to the coming Messiah in *Ps 89:36,37.* One must ask, "What is being preserved?" Those rulers weren't preserved, but the lineage God established was. In God's perfect order, establishing something includes preserving it. Keeping it. God is preserving for us our path, our work, our service to Him. Unworthy as we are, God's plan is to establish our eternal security and then to preserve our work in Him, through Him and for Him. Sometimes it's hard to recognize, given the nature of following God's plans, that what we do to serve God has lasting, even eternal ramifications. We have insight into how that can be when God spoke through Isaiah, "For as the rain and snow come down from heaven and do not return there but water the earth, making it bring forth and sprout, giving seed to the sower and bread to the eater, so shall my word be that goes out from my mouth; it shall not return to me empty, but it shall accomplish that which I purpose, and shall succeed in the thing for which I sent it." *Isa 55:10-11.* We tend to envision that statement to mean 'when I share the gospel or quote scripture, that's conclusive enough to guarantee the results I'm seeking.' First of all, that God has someone sow doesn't mean

God must have the same worker reap the harvest. Second, falling into a result-based gratification structure can lead to unhealthy efforts to do more outside of God's plan. We can wow crowds by memorizing whole chapters of scripture and quote every appropriate Bible reference but God must water after we sow. The process is entirely dependent on Him. So just make sure you're sowing the field God wants you to be working in. But really, the entire Bible is what He has spoken. It is the written embodiment of Jesus Christ. See *Jn 1:1-14.* For our part, we can speak it, proclaim it, preach it, but more importantly we must live it. In fact, we speak it, proclaim it and preach it as we live it. If not, then we're proclaiming our own gospel by our actions. It's the path lived and spoken through and for Christ that God preserves. The life of the parent that's a Godly example for the children. The friend who gives Godly advice. The boss who leads by biblical principles. It will not return to God empty, it shall succeed in the thing for which He sent it. He has equipment for us to help along the way - "The Armor of God." But more on that later. "Emperor Augustus established the first professional military medical corps, which attracted professional Greek doctors by granting rights of full Roman citizenship, tax exemptions and retirement pensions. This medical corps formed one of the first dedicated field surgery units, created well-designed sanitation systems to ward off disease and pioneered both the hemostatic tourniquet to stop hemorrhaging and to shut arteries for suturing. Camp doctors stood at the empire's medical vanguard by absorbing new ideas through their travels and studying human anatomy while performing surgeries on wounded soldiers in field hospitals. Thanks in part to the innovations of ancient Rome's medical corps, the life expectancy of the average soldier was five years longer than that of the average citizen." Christopher Klein *8 Fascinating Facts about Ancient Roman Medicine.* Roman commanders understood part of their job was to preserve their men. Not entirely for altruistic reasons, it was in their best interest as they needed the men to fulfill their ambitions. Despite popular teaching in American churches today, for the Christ follower, having our eternity secured doesn't translate to a smooth sail through life. There will be mental, emotional and physical injuries or even worse. Consider the five missionaries who went to the Huaorani Indians in Ecuador to follow the path God prepared for them. They were all speared to death by the ones to whom God sent them. They sowed but they didn't reap. Yet the word as they lived it didn't return back to God empty. Family members, including wives and a daughter of these five missionaries, went back to the same tribe and reaped the harvest that the men went seeking. Elisabeth Elliot, wife of Jim, one of the five slain men, was one that went back to live among the Huaorani, and wrote a book, "*The Savage My*

Kinsman" about God's work and her path that was part of it. Because of sin, we'll struggle daily with the warfare of our will against God's will even as we follow the direction of God down the path He prepared for us. When a vessel is set to use, it's not guaranteed to remain unbroken. But once it's used, the water or grain it carried has given nourishment to the user and that can never be undone. It will not return for repair void of having been useful in its purpose. It shall succeed in the thing for which He sent it. But God is also the master healer; Jehovah-Rapha. As the psalmist sings, "He heals the brokenhearted and binds their wounds." *Ps 147:3.* He never changes, that verse will always be true. As God has designed our bodies to heal according to His laws of physics, the emotional and spiritual wounds received during spiritual warfare can be healed by our commander and Master-Healer. Someone who is living outside of God's plan cuts themselves off from the only source of spiritual healing. To be sure, it's not that God can't but that person simply won't take themselves to the healer. And the reason is that to go to Jehovah-Rapha is also to recognize His Lordship. Some people get so deceived in spiritual warfare that they would rather ignore or even reject the healing they need because of an unwillingness to recognize God is the Alpha and Omega of their hope.

5. Fulfillment – The final component of God directing our paths is that we experience a

sense of fulfillment with our service to Him. Yes, Elohim the all powerful One considers it part of His process to want us to be satisfied with our service to Him. Psalm 112 sings about the person who delights greatly in the commandments of the Lord. Among many things the song describes, "He shall not be afraid of evil tidings: his heart is fixed, trusting in the Lord. His heart is established, *Kun,* he shall not be afraid *Ps 112:7,8.* Here our word *Kun* describes a sense of well being, according to Spiros Zodhiates, that's part of the bigger process of God directing our path. This well-being is apportioned to the one who is happily serving God. King David sang about it too in Psalm 37. He said to trust in the Lord and act like it by doing things that are pleasing to God, *vs 3.* And says later, the steps of this good person are ordered by the Lord and that this person delights in His way, *vs 23.* This person literally finds pleasure and is well-pleased with following the path of seeking first the kingdom of God. King David also mentions the challenges and benefits of following God as we previously mentioned. He says of the good man "though he fall, he shall not be cast headlong, for the Lord upholds his hand." Jehovah-Rapha, the Lord that heals is holding our hand through the difficult times. David is describing a sense of satisfaction and contentment in the process of God directing our path, even through the troubled times. Even

Moses prayed about this. "And let the beauty of the Lord our God be upon us: and establish thou the work of our hands upon us." Here Moses is actually praying that God call us into the work He has planned for us. Direct our path, Lord. Lead us into our priesthood. If the strategy of our military campaign of spiritual warfare is for God to direct our paths, then Moses says, a manifestation of that will be that the beauty of the Lord be upon us: literally the delight, grace and pleasantness of the Lord be upon us. We need this. No where else in the world can be found this kind of satisfaction.

It's pretty simple. A life under the leadership of Christ is on par with the experience of the military community. God wants us to follow Him. To be sensitive to His direction through the guidance of the Holy Spirit. And He wants us, without reservation, to be committed to Him. There is no point in holding back. King David ponders the wisdom of God, "O Lord, you have searched me and known me! You know when I sit down and when I rise up; you discern my thoughts from afar. You search out my path and my lying down and are acquainted with all my ways. Even before a word is on my tongue, behold, O Lord, you know it altogether. You hem me in, behind and before, and lay your hand upon me. Such knowledge is too wonderful for me; it is high; I cannot attain it." *Ps 139: 1-6.* It's almost laughable how little we know of ourselves compared to the knowledge God has of us.

When do we relent and defer to God in attaining our best life? Early Christians called it "The Way." The life in Christ.

Through the Gospel of Christ, our God - Jehovah-Sabaoth - the Lord of Armies leads us in a more complete and perfect way than even the example of the Roman commander. His promise to establish our paths requires a level of complexity we can't fathom and it includes our past, present and future. Our success in spiritual warfare is based on the promises of God, which are accessible through the work of Christ and grounded in the ministry of the Holy Spirit.

CHAPTER 5

TRAINING

"Their battle drills are no different from
the real thing... It would not be far from
the truth to call their drill bloodless
battles, their battles bloody drills."
Josephus *The Wars of the Jews.*

The recruitment of a new soldier, according to Michael
Simkins in *Caesar's Legions,* came only following a
character examination, as well as the expected medical
and physical testing. They were then sent with the rest of
the men assigned to their legion to specialized training
camps. Some of the men, based on their background or
interest, were taught the arts of medicine or engineering.

The rest of them, Vegetius, the ancient Roman writer
says, learned the basics of how to march, at normal pace
and quick pace, in formation. They found themselves
marching 20 miles a day in full gear at the normal pace
and 24 miles per day at quick pace. In fact, they'd soon
realize they could march as much as 50 miles in a day;
things they never thought they could do. They learned

how to carry their kit pole in the left hand, and adjust the hanging belt of their shield so it could be used properly, as well as the adjustments of the helmet, shoes, breastplate and sword scabbard so it all fit properly. It was excellent equipment that was supplied to the legions. Once it was in place, it did its job, but one must first learn how to wear it and use it.

Upon arrival at the camp, each man was assigned to an eight-man squad called, *a contuburnium*. These eight men lived together, sleeping in a large sheep skin tent. They cooked together, helped one another in all ways, and eventually would protect and keep each other alive. The recruits became proficient in helping their bunk-mates dress into the armor and likewise the proper movements that allowed others to help dress him. It had to be done quickly and efficiently so as to be prepared for the most dire of emergencies; being unexpectedly overtaken by the enemy whilst not being mounted in their armor.

There was instruction on how to build a fortified camp. Any time the legion marched to a new location, it built another fortified camp. As the ancient historian Polybius describes, "one simple plan of camp being adopted at all times and in all pieces." Each man was allocated a camp tool. Either a shovel, a turf cutter or a pick-ax became part of their marching kit along with a four-foot palisade stake which, when all the stakes were used together, made the final obstacle on the top of the palisade wall. While some dug ditches and some constructed the fortified gates, others foraged for water and wood and in so doing, everyone participated in fulfilling the commander's plan to have a well supplied place that was safe from the enemy.

In keeping with Paul's illustration, one can see the parallel to how this dynamic also works in the church.

But they were there to learn how to fight. Six foot vertical posts were used as the target, and they practiced fighting against it with wooden swords and wicker shields similar in shape but twice the weight of their standard issue equipment. Experienced soldiers instructed the preferred techniques with sword and shield. They learned to balance themselves using precise footing positions with their new combat shoes, while practicing the motions of single combat.

Fighting techniques taught the soldiers to not only be highly skilled in their aptitude of single combat, but to do so with complete dependence on their fellow soldiers – *commilitones*. Each man was taught to allow two or three feet between the men on either side. This allowed freedom of movement in the Roman fighting style. Yet he depended on those beside and behind him for protection, so he could focus on the enemy in front of him. He would also draw strength from those around him. They were after all, the ones he lived with and built bonds with through carrying a common burden; that being the life of a Roman soldier. A life of adventure, danger, rigorous assignments that test mind and body, and above all, commitment to whom they serve.

Clearly Josephus attests to the rigor of legionary training, but it wasn't something just for the raw recruits. Once the fresh troops arrived at their assigned units, the training continued so as to maintain their effectiveness, whether they were in garrison or on campaign, until their discharge from service. The soldiers understood the necessity of it. Their lives depended on it. They might even have been thankful that they were given the means and opportunity to do so by their commander. The commanders understood the return-on-investment, of the expense of constant training.

Julius Caesar records the following experience in *The Gallic Wars* when being suddenly attacked by a great multitude of Belgian tribesmen; "Much of [the normal preparations for battle] could not be done in the short time left available by the enemy's swift onset." He describes the soldiers as being "so pushed for time by the enemy's eagerness to fight that they could not even take the covers off their shields..." Caesar describes for us how this sudden and desperate incident was overcome. "But the situation was saved by two things - first, the knowledge and experience of the soldiers, whose training in earlier battles enabled them to decide for themselves what needed doing, without waiting to be told; secondly the order which Caesar had issued... not to leave the work, but to stay each with his own legion until the camp fortifications were completed..." These people were so familiar with the battlefield environment, and so prepared to endure the stresses associated with it, that they weren't distracted from the priorities of response and actions which they had previously learned and were required for success. It was clear to all, including the enemy, that the training and even the experience of previous struggles, paved the way for this success. Also, it was recognized as key to this success that everyone was in the company of those they could depend on, so that no one was caught alone in an unpredictable environment. This also capitalized on proven links of commitment that were previously established so in this unexpected event no hesitation of trust was even considered.

Success in most any endeavor requires preparation. An army can't win a battle without comprehensive plans of preparation. Nor can anyone expect success in spiritual warfare or to win any spiritual battle without a plan – a training regimen. It just won't happen by accident. The enemy is too strong for that.

What does this training look like for the modern Christ-follower? As with the Roman soldier of Paul's day, it involves several elements of activity that will prepare the way for victory. All of the elements of preparation lead to the same point – which is to make one capable of succeeding, even prospering, yet even thriving in the midst of the strife of spiritual warfare.

Train for Success

There are basic skills. The Roman soldier learned to march and learned the meaning of the commands he was given in his new military environment. For those recently reborn in Christ, Paul says there is information in the Bible that he describes as milk for a baby. That is, knowledge and disciplines that are important for the building of a solid foundation in a new life, with a new Christ-centric worldview. It's basic training for the new believer. Why Paul described it like that is explained in the profound conversation between Jesus himself and Nicodemus the scholarly priest of the Sanhedrin.

In the words of Jesus himself, "Truly, truly, I say to

you, unless one is born again he cannot see the kingdom of God."

But Nicodemus in all his studious wisdom reckoned this in the mind of the flesh, not of the Spirit, "How can a man be born when he is old? Can he enter a second time into his mother's womb and be born?"

Jesus persisted with a better foundation to interpret Godly wisdom: "unless one is born of water and the Spirit, he cannot enter the kingdom of God. That which is born of the flesh is flesh, and that which is born of the Spirit is spirit."

In this dialogue The Lord explains that the first step of our salvation: the justification of past sin, begins at a finite moment in time in which we are changed forever. Matthew Henry describes it as being "born *anothen*, which signifies both *denuo—again*, and *desuper—from above.*" Quite literally we are reborn from above. And this is only accomplished by the Holy Spirit as Matthew Henry further explains, "that is, of the Spirit working like water," regarding God cleansing our sin through the transformation of the Holy Spirit.

What are the basic training knowledge and disciplines of the reborn life? If possible we could ask Jesus what are the most important responsibilities of the believer, but someone already did that for us. He was a lawyer among the Sanhedrin.

"Teacher, which is the great commandment in the Law?"

And Jesus said to him, "You shall love the Lord your God with all your heart and with all your soul and with all your mind. This is the great and first commandment.

And a second is like it: You shall love your neighbor as yourself." *MT 22:36-40*

Jesus shared with us unequivocally what is important to God. More than just mere words, if they become part of the reborn person, they are a foundation on which to build a new life. They will affect who we are, what we do and how we think.

Once reborn in the Spirit of God and cognizant of the foundation of the 'great commandment,' a manifestation of the new life will be 'fruits of the spirit' that God expects to see from us. "But the fruit of the Spirit is love, joy, peace, patience, kindness, goodness, faithfulness, gentleness, self-control" *Gal 5:22*. How do I implement them in my life? This is part of the training of the believer. Unfortunately many who experience the saving grace of Christ cling to old habits and lifestyles, and in doing so deny the transformative power of God in their lives. Indeed the mere desire to embody the fruits of the Spirit can be all God wants to see to unleash the miracles of a transformed life.

As training continues, the soldier learns to use the tools with which his commander has equipped him. Likewise the believer learns the use of 'the Armor of God' and in doing so begins to learn by experience not only that it's safe to trust God, but also that our unchanging God is perfectly dependable to keep His Word. They learn who is God, what has He done in the past and what He says about the future. The Bible is full of the names of God. David Jeremiah of Turning Point Ministries offers 26 names of God in the Old Testament, all describing different attributes. And that's before we consider the distinctions of the Trinity, or our Messiah. David Jeremiah says "It matters" to learn about YHWH, the One who is, the self-existent One. And it all leads us to success in our struggles.

Like the Roman soldier learns individual skills of conduct and fighting, so the Christ follower learns to emulate the morals and character of Christ, and thereby, to stand in the strife of spiritual warfare. Paul explains to the Philippian believers, "Have this mind among yourselves, which is yours in Christ Jesus, who, though He was in the form of God, did not count equality with God a thing to be grasped, but emptied himself, by taking the form of a servant, being born in the likeness of men. And being found in human form, he humbled himself by becoming obedient to the point of death, even death on a cross." *Phi 2:5-8*. The Creator took the form of His creation. In paving the way for redemption, Jesus the Christ also gave us a perfect example of how to live in the flesh. How He lived: that's God's expectation for us. If one were to describe His conduct in list form with bullet points, one might come to the law of Moses. However, Jesus' Roman execution by crucifixion, something otherwise impossible unless He willingly allowed it, along with His breaking the bonds of death three days later, instituted a new code of conduct. One that accounts for our inability to meet God's expectations perfectly. One that values more our heart's commitment to Him, than any act of service towards Him. The gospel writer says He was "full of grace and truth". But there is more and God has preserved in scripture, everything we need to know about the life of Jesus. It should be our life's goal to emulate who He is. We must train, with the help of God's Holy Spirit, to that end.

While honing these individual skills, a life was developed within the legion, that required supporting fellow soldiers. Success or failure of every individual utterly depended on it. The commander incubated the environment in which that could happen. For many, this particular aspect of our life in Christ is easy to dismiss. "I don't need the church to have God." That's true in the most basic sense, but in the words of Tom Hall of Kerygma Ventures, "God doesn't create any lone rangers for the Kingdom of God." If that's true, and it is, then one does need the church to live the best life God has planned for them.

Train with your Commilitones

From the start, the legion's new recruits are trained by those with experience in serving their commander. God's plan is quite the same. Yes, we have direct access to God. We commune with God through prayer. Yet Jesus in His prayer to the Father *Jn 17* "strongly expresses concern for the welfare of His followers, He speaks of the unity between the Father and the Son as a model for the unity of believers with one another." Millard J. Erickson *Christian Theology*. Although that's quite the model, and it speaks to the type of relationship believers might experience, we can see this too in Paul's same words to the Philippians where he gets into more detail on what this looks like, "So if there is any encouragement in Christ, any comfort from love, any participation in the Spirit, any affection and sympathy, complete my joy by being of the same mind, having the same love, being in full accord and of one mind. Do nothing from selfish ambition or conceit, but in humility count others more significant than yourselves. Let each of you look not only to his own interests, but also to the interests of others. Have this mind among yourselves, which is yours in Christ Jesus, who, though he was in the form of God, did not count equality with God a thing to be grasped" *Phil 2:1-6*. We should be considering our existence within the community of the church, considering the well being of others, and doing so with humility similar to what Jesus exemplified for us by taking the form of His creation. Paul also is saying that our connection to the body of Christ is directly related to the impact of God in our lives. Paul speaks specifically of encouragement, comfort, affection and sympathy.

"As iron sharpens iron, so a man sharpens the countenance of his friend" *Pr 27:17 NKJV*. Examining this along with Philippians 2 gives us a picture not unlike that of the Roman soldier. A believer having lived for years seeing how God works; how true are God's promises and how fulfilling are God's provisions, then encourages the new believer in 'the way' of following the Lord – helping to prepare for spiritual warfare. Compatriots discuss the importance and benefits of following commands. Men of the *contubernium* share food, not allowing anyone to go hungry. Every day one wakes up, they share the common goals of serving their commander wherever He leads.

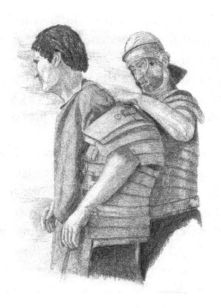

How integral is this unity of believers to our success as disciples of Christ? Jesus gave the instruction: "A new commandment I give to you, that you love one another: just as I have loved you, you also are to love one another. By this all people will know that you are my disciples, if you have love for one another." *Jn 13:34,35.* Of all the things that might matter to God, how we treat others is what will allow the world to see Jesus in us. It's key for our success in spiritual warfare to consider those around us with care and humility – to help others put on their Armor of God.

Eventually there comes a time when we realize that, like the Roman soldier, we must fight. As Jesus fought with satan in the wilderness, we must fight for our holiness and integrity. Like the nation of Israel after crossing the

Jordan River, we too must fight for whatever it is that God has planned for us. We could live in complacency and unbelief, wandering around in the wilderness until following generations seize the will of God, as they did who walked out of captivity in Egypt. Or we could realize the fullness of God in our lives and follow Him. The choice is ours.

We saw how Julius Caesar regarded the soldiers' training and previous engagements as crucial to their success in the most desperate of moments. It is possible that christians can be equally prepared to respond with alacrity in those crucial moments of spiritual warfare. A Roman soldier operates in the power of his commander. This power grows out of the confidence he gains from what he learns about his commander, his penchant to develop skills as instructed and willingness to follow orders. This suggests then, the more we learn about our commander the Lord of Hosts (literally of armies), the more we can operate in His power. It also suggests that if we receive the equipage and instruction from the Lord that He offers us, we'd be prepared for the experiences He has planned for us. Though there is no doubt that at times the legionnaires endured their training with drudgery, there was no question as to its value. Do we consider receiving instruction from the Lord with the same value? The Bible contains all the instruction we need, to prepare us to operate in the power of God through the Holy Spirit. The attention we give to the word of God will have the greatest impact on our conduct during the rigors of spiritual warfare. It affects how we respond to unforeseen difficulties, our behavior when interacting with others, our personal goals and our expectations of others and things we experience.

Train Rigorously

As God's path is different for everyone, so is God's training different for everyone. Some people read their Bible first thing every morning seeking instruction from God. Maybe that works for you, maybe it doesn't, but it's an expectation of God that you seek a training regimen for the crucial growth you'll need to fulfill His plan for you. Starting with the milk (foundational wisdom) of God's word, then growing as God told Isaiah *Isa 28:10*, precept upon precept, until we become a spiritual centurion in the host of the Lord, feared by and invincible (in God's strength) to the enemies of God.

However, regardless of the details of the training regimen, there should be a pursuit of specific results. Using the legionary model of training, the Christian can glean some principles regarding the expected goals for every trainee. They should develop a familiarity with the tools and equipment given by the commander. One should advance in the skills of employing all of the endowments of the commander. This includes everything from how to best use the food rations to building expertise in the use of the armor. Most soldiers even going as far as using their salary to embellish the armor they receive from the commander, thus showing a substantial commitment to their life in the legion. Lastly, the training should provide understanding of the commander's goals, and the expectations of one's performance. The trainee performs this training knowing that the ultimate purpose of it is to improve one's ability to meet the commander's expectation.

As training gradually becomes more rigorous for the new legionary recruit, we see a parallel in the parables of Jesus. God imparts to us some small responsibility in following His will, after which there is either a stagnation in our relationship with God or a growth into greater responsibilities (and blessings).

This is not based on success or failure, but on how we process the results with regard to our walk with God. The commander is always responsible for the results. A soldier may smart from a defeat or rejoice in a victory, but the commander is the one who gives account for the results. In fact, the only time soldiers answer for the results is when they disobey the orders of the commander. Jehovah–Sabaoth, the righteous leader, and perfectly just commander is not only responsible for the results of an action, but also holds us equally to account for obedience. Like the Roman soldier, we honor our Commander for the victories, because of His leadership, guidance, training and provision. The author of 1ˢᵗ Peter suggests that we should be serving God in the strength of God and thus He be honored by the results of an action.

Perhaps the greatest benefit of following God through this process of spiritual warfare, is that there actually is no failure. Our Commander is El Shaddai, the all sufficient God almighty. The gospel writer reminds us "God is spirit" *Jn 4:24*. As a consequence of this spiritual nature, He is infinite and omnipotent, as Paul describes, "The God who made the world and everything in it, being

Lord of heaven and earth, does not live in temples made by man" *Acts14:24.* When one ponders the nature of God, we might not consider it much as miracles go, when God manipulates the laws of physics He created. More that we marvel at His willingness to do so. Millard J. Erickson describes this nature of God as "in terms of space, there is no place where He cannot be found." And further, "nowhere within the creation is God not accessible."

Yet the God of these lofty attributes is the same who ensures "all things work together for good, for those who are called according to his purpose." *Rom 8:28.* This is true especially as applied to spiritual warfare. Success or failure, victory or loss nor results of any kind affect the dependability of that promise from God. The reason this is possible is because as Timothy Keller states, "God, perfect and omnipotent, wants for nothing. His power transcends materialism. And because of the power of God in us, our wants can transcend materialism too." And not just materialism, but any of the cares of the world. From concerns over our physical well being to the myriad onslaughts by the enemy on our mental, emotional or spiritual health, the power of God transcends them all. Therefore God isn't bothered by failure or loss.

Consider Joseph's reaction to being dealt so unjustly by his own brothers. Is there any question this is a most desperate example of spiritual warfare? Many people have strained relations at times with their siblings, but how would it affect one's walk with God to literally be sold into slavery in a foreign country by siblings? This was God's unexpected plan for Joseph. It involved many hardships over many years, yet Joseph could see God's hand in the experience. People do bad things as a result of sin, but God works on behalf of "those who are called according to His purpose." Joseph was so confident in His Lord, that he trusted the work God was doing in him and through him even in such a difficult experience. "As for you, you meant evil against me, but God meant it for good, to bring it about that many people should be kept alive, as they are today." *Gen 50:20*. As Joseph was tied up, thrown in a cage and hauled off to Egypt, he had no idea what God was preparing, but his faith-based conduct through the years of struggle (even after he gained favor with Pharaoh, he lived with the reality of being forcefully cast out and separated from his family) is what God used to save many people from famine.

God is more concerned about how we process the experiences of spiritual warfare and specifically the nature of our love and commitment to Him amidst the conflict. God's promise guarantees that there will always - without exception - be some benefit and value to the experience, regardless of the difficulty and pain of the loss or lack of completion of a task. It might be silly or commonplace to say simply "learn from our mistakes." It is however very true that not even the greatest of commanders can talk their raw recruits through the process of guaranteeing success in conflict. Instead, the commander creates training environments that help them overcome the demands of combat.

Once the untried soldier survives a battle, he sees how dependable his commander is, how reliable is the equipment he received from his commander and how valuable the training he experienced. Having survived conflict, the soldier also realizes why the commander nurtures a system of codependency with the *commilitones*, and the associated benefits of support and safety. Then he can more confidently follow the commander into the next event. These experiences become a most valuable part of a continued training process, no matter the outcome, because of God's promise to always be working on our behalf.

CHAPTER 6

THE ENEMY

"The Roman method of fighting was...
tested and tempered on many battlefields
against all varieties of foe."
Donald Featherstone *'Warriors and
Warfare in Ancient and Medieval Times.'*

Upon admission into the legion, the recruit knew not
where he would go. Not just that one never knows what
the future holds, but specifically that the functions of
empire would call him into the unknown. Admission
meant subordination of self to the interests of the kingdom.

Before donning the uniform, the individual lived
a presumably quiet life with nothing more than the
usual challenges. Upon entrance into the legion, he was
transformed into a new person according to the will of
his commander, he was trained with new knowledge and
armed with new equipment. Suddenly he became a threat
to the enemies of Rome.

These enemies were on the fringes of the empire's
borders and they were also found within: those who sought

to steal from the abundance of Rome and its people, and destroy the vitality of the kingdom. By strength and wisdom the enemies were held back and the *pax romana* 'Roman peace' maintained.

The enemies of Rome were as diverse as they were numerous. They were blue-faced tribesmen of Scotland. They were tall Germans, who along with the Celts of western Europe, towered over the legionnaires. So great was the disparity of stature between them and the Italian soldiers that Caesar records during the siege of Alesia, the city inhabitants stood on the high walls taunting the Romans below, calling them pygmies. There were the cavalrymen of North Africa and the Greek hoplite infantry that fought in dense formations with spears 8-20 feet in length, according to Victor Davis Hanson in *The Wars of the Ancient Greeks*. Jewish revolutionaries in the province of Judea, some calling themselves the messiah, stirred strife not just for the Romans but also as Josephus tells us in *The Wars of the Jews*, committing indignities upon their own local populace. Large groups of pirates hunting the Mediterranean Sea were a major threat to the economy of the empire until legionnaires-turned-marines completely eliminated the threat. And there were always the highway robbers throughout the empire lurking in the vast network of Roman roads, whose efforts were curtailed by police units of soldiers garrisoned strategically to aid freedom of commerce.

Notwithstanding this array of enemies, all with their distinctions of weaponry and fighting styles, there is one form of combat for the Romans to deter these diverse threats. The typical Roman citizen developed discipline and independence within the greater community of citizenship of the empire, likewise the soldiers were trained to use tools of individual combat whilst protecting their nearby comrades. This is in contrast to the various tribesmen who fought solely for themselves, seeking personal glory over their peers while giving little heed to their comrades. These usually fought with great flourishes of slashing longswords made all the more flamboyant by their great stature. The various peoples of the eastern Mediterranean rooted in Greek culture fought huddled together in formations, called a *phalanx*, packed so tightly that their shields overlapped leaving a hedge of spears sticking out the front row of the shield-wall. With this the Romans would, after launching their javelins to upset the enemy formation, march up and smash off the pointed spearheads with their sturdy sword, then move into the *phalanx* with ease whilst the Greeks were too close to their comrades to even pull their sword out of its sheath. Romans had the propensity to take the offensive in battle because they were so confident in their training and commanders. So they developed a shield that was much more than simply something to hide behind. We'll see what that looks like in 'Part 2 The Armor of God.'

The important factor is, the Romans understood their threats so well that they could create one set of tools and the appropriate strategies that afforded them overwhelming success. What might have happened if they also had an all-knowing and omnipotent Roman commander?

Yes, we can imagine that because that's what God's people have. What a tactical advantage that our Captain has already numbered the hairs on the head of every single one of our enemies, and while we confront enemies in spiritual warfare that enjoy complete autonomy because the Lord allows it, He knows them perfectly because He created them too.

This may be confusing for some because, as we have seen, while God is always working for 'those who are called according to His purpose,' it may be misunderstood that God should be undermining all the efforts of all our enemies. But God didn't promise a life where He makes all our problems go away. "This is what the wicked are like—always free of care" *Ps 73*:12. *El Elyon* the most high God is no more interested in controlling His enemies than He is in controlling His own people. This would make for a world full of automatons where God is merely a puppet-master. Christ followers usually find success through the ministrations of the Holy Spirit in their lives (perhaps by the grace of wisdom or the blessing of peace), and not as commonly by seeing walls crumble before them. Often it's the Lord's preparation of the heart, for events God sees coming long before the Christian has the slightest hint of the future. Or it's the comforting strength of Jehovah-Shammah, the Lord our Comforter, that gives endurance through tragedy as with Paul during the struggles of his missionary journeys.

Rome's commanders weren't successful because they could affect the enemy, but because of the influence they had on their own men who followed them. As Keith Green, the evocative preacher/musician of the 1970's and 80's explained in an interview with 100 Huntley Street TV:

Interviewer, "How did you know Jesus was God?'

Keith, "He proved it to me."

"How?"

"He changed me. That was the greatest miracle He could have done. I could have seen, ya know, Mount Everest skipping across the United States and jump into the ocean, and that wouldn't have done as much for me as Him changing me."

That God could satisfy a fully autonomous individual capable of independent thought, who is moreover naturally disposed to be contrary to Him, to be completely changed by the grace and mercy of the Lord is as Keith Green said, the greatest miracle. This transformation with the singular focus of Jesus Christ as our foundation, is what undermines the diverse strength of our enemies in spiritual warfare.

Who are They?

So who exactly are our enemies? For the legionnaire, his enemies were clear. In spiritual warfare our enemies are equally distinguishable. "For we do not wrestle against flesh and blood, but against the rulers, against the authorities, against the cosmic powers over this present darkness, against the spiritual forces of evil in the heavenly places." *Eph 6:12.* We must be careful here, adhering to the written word of God to avoid missteps into doctrines of worldly mysticism. Let's clarify now: we believe God is who He said He is. God created satan. Satan is a real, tangible part of creation not unlike anything else we see God made. Satan chose a path contrary to God's desire and has a personality that we must reckon with, and that we'll see more about shortly. That's it.

First Paul reminds us that we're not fighting against flesh and blood. Although we often see flesh and blood: an actual person doing us harm, Paul wants us to clearly understand that it's not the flesh and blood we're contending with. There is always a spiritual inspiration from one of the enemies of God behind the action we're seeing from the flesh and blood. For example, is this person someone who doesn't know God? Then he's doing what is natural to himself, being without the comfort and guidance of the Holy Spirit. That reality doesn't make the evil we confront acceptable, but it helps us understand the nature of the fight. So we're in fact not just fighting flesh and blood but then the issue becomes; that which is against God contending with that of the kingdom of God.

Does this require one to stand on the principles of God to stem the progress of evil in the world? Or does it require Christlike compassion to participate with God in diverting a soul away from the grips of separation from God?

Is the flesh and blood we're seeing a Christ follower? Are they acting in accordance with God's expectations?

Am I acting thus?

These questions are all a matter of spiritual warfare. They help us recognize the enemy.

Often we're reluctant to admit that the root of a particular struggle is not just the flesh and blood we see in the mirror, but our own nature which is so contrary to God that it continues to trouble us even on our God-ordained path.

Suddenly all the commonplace daily experiences aren't just random problems, but matters of spiritual warfare which, by their nature, affect the kingdom of God. No matter what, the right response can only be affected through the wisdom of God accessed via the Holy Spirit abiding in us. Additionally, we're often encouraged to come to this holy wisdom by the council of Christ-like people who are familiar with the nature of spiritual warfare.

Paul goes on to articulate, if not flesh and blood, what we actually fight against. Knowing the enemy will quickly indicate to the soldier the nature of the fight. Fighting a German tribesman? Be prepared to plant one's feet firmly and thrust the sword upward. Fighting a Greek phalanx? Be prepared to use arm strength to parry the spearheads and push into the shield wall. In *Christian Theology* Millard J. Erickson paraphrases the sources that may lead us astray as, "evil spirits, other men or oneself."

Paul describes the power of *arche* – the local government. This is not to suggest God expects us to be fundamentally *Anarchist*, but to recognize that the will of a society made up of individuals who are born into opposition to God, is then, collectively and fundamentally opposed to the will of the Lord. While we welcome and support the rule of law organized by the *arche* and the peace it affords, we must be mindful of the efforts of society to lead us away from our relationship with and worship of God.

Within the description of this enemy we can not only recognize the collective efforts of a society void of God to be contentious, but also the peer pressure of individuals. God doesn't expect us to hide in the recesses of the church, but to be involved with the world around us. It's here that this enemy seeks conflict and here we can find success in spiritual warfare. Jesus said: "You are the light of the world. A city set on a hill cannot be hidden. Nor do people light a lamp and put it under a basket, but on a stand, and it gives light to all in the house. In the same way, let your light shine before others," The Holy Spirit that lives in us is the light in a dark world. This light emits itself as the fruits of the Spirit. Love, joy, peace, patience, kindness, generosity, faithfulness, gentleness, self control. It's not us, but God in us, and just like the candlelight in a dark house, it's beneficial to everyone in the house. Jesus even stated the purpose of bearing this "light" in a dark world: "so that they may see your good works and give glory to your Father who is in heaven." This is why we don't hide the lamp under a basket, why we don't need to hide who we are in Christ, because we want to bring attention to how special it is to experience the fruits of

God's blessing. So that what is seen in us can contribute to the recognition that any goodness in the world finds its source in Elohim-the All Powerful Creator.

Paul also describes as an enemy, *poneria - malicious depravity, plots to sin, iniquity, wickedness*. Here is Paul speaking of the performance of actions contrary to the will of God, but specifically, the very intent to do so. The malicious nature and plots that lead to the action. Not so much the sin, but the willfulness to it. This is our nature. We're born into it. For the believer in Christ, His sacrifice mercifully cleans our record in the eyes of God. Nonetheless it is still the nature we possess that we contend with, that is an enemy to us in spiritual warfare. Someday it won't be, but meanwhile if we desire to be a person that's pleasing to God, we must fight to subdue the nature we inherited from the first Adam. If we're to reap the benefits of a life obedient to God, we must rely on the strength of God to overcome our impulses to rebel against His will.

With this enemy in particular, it's helpful to recognize when facing it. Jesus said we should approach God with child-like faith. That is, with an honesty lacking the inhibitions of adulthood. Perhaps we should look at our potential for rebellion against God (that's all sin is) with a similarly child-like nature. That is without pride, or embarrassment, or selfishness, or deceit, or maliciousness. Since God sees through all that, we might as well be honest with ourselves and take into account God's view of the situation.

While we might contend with other enemies over which we have no control, when fighting this enemy, our own nature – rebellious against God, this is the one enemy we can control. Especially if we're seeking God's help. Paul reminds us: "No temptation has overtaken you that is not common to man. God is faithful, and he will not let you be tempted beyond your ability, but with the temptation he will also provide the way of escape, that you may be able to endure it." *1 Cor 10:13.* Let's be clear on the message here. It does not declare that "God will not give me more than I can handle." Given the frailties of human nature, it's likely that we'll come in contact with more than we can endure, and often. However, God "will not let" us succumb to our frailties because "He will also provide" a means to overcome the enticement of rebellion and the pain of the conflict. This may mean, as Paul says, "enduring" via divine strength in the face of a struggle, or the provision of a countermovement from the temptation. As we'll soon see, either of these are purposeful tactics in spiritual warfare. In this God is faithful. He is perfectly faithful. He will never disappoint the hope of His children or abandon them to their own devices if they're seeking His help. Thus the decision to act outside of God's expectations is always a choice. Sometimes a difficult or even sacrificial one, but always a choice.

Lastly and predictably, Paul lists *kosmokrator* as an enemy to be recognized. According to James Strong in his concordance, this is "an epithet of satan." What do we know about this enemy? To answer this, we might be best served by using caution in the sources from which we draw. Much conjecture has found its way into the biblical narrative. In particular the prophets Isaiah and Ezekiel are attributed by some to have spoken of the chief rebel against God. While this may be true, it comes at best, by way of allegory amidst God's pronouncements against actual earthly rulers. If we focus instead on factual statements by other biblical writers, we can draw ample knowledge to understand the nature of our fight against this enemy. Whether satan is a proper name or a description, we can see he is not just an idea of something, but a real created-by-God being whom the Lord interacts with in several places in scripture.

We know satan is one of many angels that sinned and were cast down. *2 Pet 2:4*. This postulates these fallen ones were originally created and serving God, like other angels in scripture, as couriers of His pronouncements or agents of His will.

Based on Satan's involvement with Job, his temptation of Jesus and His receiving orders from God in John's Revelation, we can see him risen as leader of the host of the fallen. At this point we find the allegories of the prophets aligning with our knowledge so far of satan and the fallen, thus giving perhaps some credibility to the connection.

We see the fallen ones have an earthly presence and a spiritual presence in heaven and hell. They interact with people on earth, as does satan with God in heaven, and hell was created as their eternal condemnation for the rebellion.

The fallen host, under Satan's leadership, are in a continuous state of insurrection against the kingdom of God. "Your adversary the devil prowls around like a roaring lion, seeking someone to devour." *1Pet 5:8*.

Paul advises Timothy that a key attribute of satan is conceit. "He must not be a recent convert, or he may become puffed up with conceit and fall into the condemnation of the devil." *1Tim 3:6*. That is, high-mindedness and pride. To consider oneself better than others in an immoral way. Seeing satan as a created being by God with the same limitations as any other creation, we can understand better how freewill led to rebellion. Observing other examples might give us more insight. Adolf Hitler for example, after accumulating unimaginable power, allowed conceit to fester into arrogance that led to his destruction. He literally could no longer see reality and withdrew into fantasy where facts no longer mattered as much as his desires. With such great power as what satan was given by God, perhaps he experienced a similar digression and this is why we fight an enemy that's so committed to a losing battle.

During satan's interaction with Jesus in *Mt 4* we can observe some level of power that he holds in the world. In *Heb 2:14* Paul implies satan as holding some power over death. In the Revelation, Jesus is seen holding the keys to hell, and tradition tells that during Jesus' three days of burial, He went to hell to conquer and take the keys at that time. Further reflection reveals that Jesus in no wise needed to buy his ownership of the kingdoms of the world and their glory through yielding to satan. *John 1* instructs that Jesus created it all. Apparently satan was convinced enough that he had properly usurped control of God's creation to offer the temptation to Jesus, but there is no reason to think that Jesus had to go and get the keys of hell and take control over the death experience. It's perhaps the most profound misjudgment in the history of all of creation, that satan manipulated events leading to the murder of Jesus Christ with the expectation that Jesus' death would lead to victory for himself and the fallen host. That the grave couldn't hold Him showed that satan only ever had the impression of power over death. In fact, the only tangible power he has now, is held by his ability to deceive people about what real power he lacks.

The Lord describes satan as a liar and indeed, the father of lies. "You are of your father the devil, and your will is to do your father's desires. He was a murderer from the beginning, and does not stand in the truth, because there is no truth in him. When he lies, he speaks out of his own character, for he is a liar and the father of lies." *Jn 8:44.* That is, he's the originator and leading figure in the notion of deception. Further, he and the host of fallen like to dress up and pretend they're something which they are not. "And no wonder, for even Satan disguises himself as an angel of light." *2 Cor 11:14.*

Amidst the early growth of the church, satan filled the heart of Ananias and Saphira. We can understand this to be possible by the enemy's mastery of deception and his attempts to prey on the human propensity to oppose God.

Satan likewise holds people captive, as with the woman in Luke 13. Jesus didn't heal her, He told her in *vs12* she was 'freed' a*poluo - released, set at liberty* from her disability. Jesus then told the rabbi of the local synagogue that she had been bound by satan for 18 years. With a contemporary understanding of the power of the mind and its potential impact on physical health and well being, the experience of this woman can be seen as less an adventure of fantastic mystical nature, than an interaction between two beings created by God – one seeking to deceive and the other willing to believe the lie. Consequently, Jesus supernaturally helped the woman break the cycle of deception satan had over her. She didn't have the power to do it. Jesus did.

This is not to say all illness is a result of this same experience. Although it is possible, or Jesus was lying, no need to give credit where it doesn't belong. More often it's the impact of illness, more than the illness itself that is a source of spiritual warfare.

Seeing that the rebellion commenced after the creation and sometime before the time of Eve's temptation, this enemy has spent millennia since then observing the human condition and the effects of sin. We are therefore wise to expect to confront a skilled enemy.

It's the intent of all of these enemies of God to encourage us to move in a direction away from the council and will of God. Bible writers call this "going astray" of God's expectations. This gives a mental picture of physically walking off the path of God's plans for us, which presumes a decisive moment in which the perpetrator chooses to commit the action. Jesus repeated several times in the gospels to "take heed," suggesting that the decision to either rebel or obey is not predetermined. Nay, it's quite within our grasp. Sometimes a challenge by one of these enemies is a simple choice of no great friction or sacrifice in obedience to God. However, given the nature and strength of each of these enemies, more often the battle can only be fought in the power of God, with the council of the Holy Spirit and the armor of God.

CHAPTER 7

THE FIGHT

Principles of War

"Well-disciplined, confident to the point of arrogance,"
> Donald Featherstone describes the Roman soldier in *Warriors and Warfare in Ancient and Medieval Times.*

The importance of the soldier's discipline and confidence lies in the fact that they aren't privy to the grand strategies or minutiae of tactics planned by the commander. It's logistically impossible for them to be. Without the concern of bigger issues, the soldier is occupied solely with the execution of the plans. Lucius Aemilius Paullus was the

Roman commander that defeated the Macedonian King Perseus. He told his soldiers, "For my part, I shall do my duty as a general; I shall see to it that you are given the chance of successful action. It is no duty of yours to ask what is going to happen; your duty is, when the signal is given, to play your full part as fighting men." In this it's helpful to know how the enemy prosecutes his warfare. All the enemies. This informs the soldier with his personal conduct. It helps the soldier avoid mistakes, minimizes unforeseen events and gives the soldier confidence by making the coming struggle more predictable.

For this reason, it's useful for the soldier to understand the tribesmen with whom they fought. In these cultures, the hierarchies of society and politics are formed around an individual's ability to impress and inspire confidence over the greatest number of people. Therefore individual combat was stressed for the armies of these people. To oppose them it would be important for the Roman soldier to maintain discipline in the formation. While the soldier might feel the compulsion in the midst of the conflict to be drawn out of formation into a singular combat with an enemy, it would be helpful to anticipate this temptation and therefore be easier to predetermine the choice to maintain the proper position amidst the security of comrades.

Likewise, the Greek armies are made up mostly of citizen conscriptions of agrarian societies. These soldiers equip themselves and are prepared to fight at the bidding of their commander. However they lack any boldness that might result in personal injury. They consider it better to survive a conflict to return home to their farm. Their densely formed phalanxes making offensive maneuvers difficult, battles enjoined by two Greek armies often digress to a shoving match between the phalanx formations resulting in few mortalities, and ending when one of the groups loses heart and capitulates. Armed with this knowledge, it's helpful for the Roman soldier to expect orders for sudden quick movements of aggression in battle, thereby recognizing them as an expedient means to overwhelm the slow enemy formations rather than an unpredictable and risky experiment by the commander.

These are examples of how the same Roman soldiers, with the same set of equipment, training, and methods of operation, could make slight changes to their expectations and tactics to overcome diverse enemies given some foreknowledge of the conflict.

Principles of Spiritual Warfare

Using the "General Principles" of Clausewitz discourse on strategy, he articulates three main objects to be sought. They are: 1- destroy the power of the enemy. 2- take possession of the enemy's sources of strength. 3- gain public opinion. We can use this framework to diagnose what to expect from the three enemies which we just identified and in doing so, like the Roman soldiers, modify our expectations (what we expect to see from the enemy and our commander) and tactics to realize success in spiritual warfare.

The **first object** in warfare is to destroy the power of the enemy. This 'power of the enemy' referred to here is the combat capability of a given group. This is exactly why Caesar surrounded the city of Alesia with the Celtic chieftain Vercingetorix and his army inside. Caesar wanted once and for all to destroy the combat capability of the chieftain's rebellion. In doing so Caesar would become the uncontested ruling power in western Europe.

According to Clausewitz, the means of prosecuting this path of destroying the opponent's power is to "direct our principle operations against the main body of the enemy army or at least against an important portion of his forces." This is exactly why the German double agent Arminius, led the Roman General Varus into the Teutoberg forest and ambush, resulting in the complete annihilation of three legions. The enemy wanted to destroy Rome's combat power too. The goal is to seek out the combatant components that might do harm, and remove the threat, thus clearing the way to usurp power over the opposing entity.

We know satan to be the first and foremost self-proclaimed enemy of YaHWeH. We know satan wants to be perceived as what our God actually is. That is, to be worshiped as the all powerful God. This is what he will compel the anti-christ of prophecy to proclaim, as he commits the abomination of desolation. *See Dan 9 & 2 Thess 2*. Before he can reach that goal, he has to destroy the power of YaHWeH. It's possible to better understand this particular enemy of God by considering Clausewitz's first object of warfare.

The Christian can then perceive that the primary means of satan reaching his end goal is to destroy the power of God whenever possible. It's why he is constantly roaming the earth seeking to destroy. We can therefore expect the way he does so is to seek out God's combatants that might do him harm in a sense of hindering his ability to reach the goal of usurping God's power.

Like the Roman joining the legion who immediately sets himself apart as an enemy to those who seek to destroy Rome, the believer reborn into God's grace immediately becomes a target for God's enemies. The only way a believer won't experience this enemy is if that Christian isn't a threat to him. It follows then, satan will focus his efforts on any agents of God's work. It's not a matter of if, but when. We will face God's enemies. Jesus said it's because of our association with Him. "and you will be hated by all for my name's sake." *Mt 10:22.* There have been many who consider this a scary or dangerous position in which to find themselves. Jesus actually addressed that idea further in his dialogue in Matthew 10, "And fear not them which kill the body, but are not able to kill the soul: but rather fear him which is able to destroy both soul and body in hell." Often overlooked in this statement by Jesus is that, given God's ability to be supremely most destructive, this is something that need be feared only by God's enemies. For the fact remains God has made a commitment that His people reborn into fellowship with Christ can no longer be subject to the eternally destructive power of God. For the believer, then, this statement serves to remind us that God is worth our reverential respect and obedience.

Since we know God didn't save us to be abandoned and marginalized in our life with Him, "But ye are a chosen generation, a royal priesthood, an holy nation, a peculiar people; that ye should shew forth the praises of him who hath called you out of darkness into his marvelous light" *1 Pet 2:9 KJV,* all of His people can be sure that with the priesthood work that God has planned for us, the enemy will come seeking to destroy those plans and efforts to proliferate God's influence. However, as we have seen in chapter 4, satisfaction is one of the component blessings for His people, when following His path. So it might follow then, that despite the associated difficulties with fighting God's enemies, one might actually be offended if considered a marginal threat and not persecuted for our fellowship with God. "Count it all joy, my brothers, when you meet trials of various kinds, for you know that the testing of your faith produces steadfastness. And let steadfastness have its full effect, that you may be perfect and complete, lacking in nothing." *Jas 1:2-4.* The experience of spiritual warfare is a process through which one learns about God by seeing Him in action, ideally leading to modifications of one's awareness to be more loyal, committed, dependent, reverent, thankful and enamored with and toward God.

Napoleon said that anything the enemy wants you to do, don't do it. Thereby postulating that it's good to destroy anything the enemy wants to do. So, we can expect that any of God's enemies will try to destroy anything God is doing, and anything God's people are doing for Him. If it's good for the kingdom of God, it will proliferate the power and influence of God that satan seeks to destroy. It becomes more obvious then, why even the little trials and conflicts of spiritual warfare become significant. They impact the support of God's power. From the little attacks on our integrity, to our behavior through a failure at work and everything else we experience daily, if it's important enough for God's enemies to attack it, it's important enough for us to contend.

It's worth mentioning the opposing assertion. God is working as it pleases Him, to destroy the enemy's power. Their combative power. It would be nice to single out satan for this fact, but that serves only to minimize our impression of the power of the other enemies of self and the world at large. We read John's Revelation and what's to come, and how He has a plan to conclude the matter. Meanwhile God isn't willing that any should perish (eternally) but that all come to repentance (and eternal peace with Him). *2 Pet 3*:9. This is the practical need for God's power on earth. This asserts that God's plans lead to the diminution of satan's power; all the plans God has for every one of His people. The individual priesthoods of all believers, lead to the increase of God's power and the decrease of the power of God's enemies. That's what is always at stake for our efforts in spiritual warfare.

Clausewitz considers the first and most important rule in accomplishing the objectives is to use 'the utmost energy.' He suggests that displaying any moderation might leave one short of their aim. Even considering the potential cost of victory, making every effort to achieve victory so the cost could be overcome as quickly as possible, is the best course to follow. We can be sure God's enemies hold nothing back to the prosecution of their efforts against God's kingdom and His people. We would therefore be remiss in any attempt to show moderation in our spiritual warfare. Particularly since God, the author and finisher of our faith, is so wholeheartedly concerned with our heart's inclination toward Him, and not at all concerned by our physical inability to accomplish tasks for Him. We need not concern ourselves with the difficulties in our way, but only of our commitment and obedience to Him.

In the operations to carry out the objective of destroying enemy power, the ancient Chinese general Sun Tzu said there is an art to war. That there are best practices to follow and principles to pursue. The same is very true of spiritual warfare. Although it's not as obvious that this is true, because we're not fighting against flesh and blood, but the spiritual nature of things in our warfare requires spiritual discernment from our commander more than physical sight. These insights can be built into tactics. That is, the actual actions we see of the enemy and how we contend against those actions.

One of the tactics is the 'frontal assault.' Alexander the Great perfected this tactic. His success lay in the ability to find and exploit weakness in his enemy. Sallying an attack of enough force at the decisive point of weakness serves to break the enemy's will to fight. To do this, Alexander was always watching his enemy. Opportunities presented themselves to him when a few, perhaps even a single enemy soldier moved just slightly out of formation because of terrain obstacles. Or perhaps the enemy would misjudge the situation and mistakenly place themselves in an exposed position relative to Alexander's formations (Alexander would encourage this possibility by masking his own troop disposition by moving skirmishers around in front of his army). He would then have a concentration of force, prepared ahead of time, to contact the point of weakness, causing the enemy to cease any further efforts to fight.

Yes, satan (and the fallen) can do the same thing. They are always looking for someone to catch in a weak position. Yes, he has skirmishers to confuse a given situation. In the 2nd letter to Corinth, Paul even confesses to some confrontation with a "messenger of satan" that was harassing him. God's people often find themselves in weakened positions for the same reasons. We allow our surroundings to compel us to move out from where God wants us to be. We misjudge a situation and go somewhere or do something God didn't intend.

Here it's important to grasp the key element to our part of this experience. We've established that our ability to complete a task for God is not required. In all honesty God can supernaturally ignore the laws of physics He created. And He has access to many very committed disciples who are very capable and experienced in receiving God's wisdom. The reality is, not only does He **not** need us, but also that He **does** want us to participate in serving Him. In fact He built His entire plan around our participation, with all our infirmities and weaknesses.

Paul even reminds us of the irrelevance of our weaknesses, to help us avoid distraction and deception from the enemy of God. "[My grace is sufficient for you, for my power is made perfect in weakness.] Therefore I will boast all the more gladly of my weaknesses, so that the power of Christ may rest upon me. For the sake of Christ, then, I am content with weaknesses, insults, hardships, persecutions, and calamities. For when I am weak, then I am strong." *2 Cor 12:9-10*. God told Paul,

God's *charis - divine influence upon the heart and its reflection in the life*, is satisfactory to the completion of the task at hand. Further, the perfection of God's omnipotence is seen in His ability to empower our success in spiritual warfare regardless of our weaknesses. "Therefore" Paul says it's beneficial to embrace our weaknesses because God wants us to recognize His *dunamis - miraculous strength*, when it brings us success. Because of this promise from God, it's possible to be content amidst the greatest of discomforts in spiritual warfare. However Paul warns the ability to do so is dependent on our willingness to honor Christ with the success since He is the one who made it possible.

Another of the tactics to observe is the 'flanking movement.' By this, is referred, the attempt to attack a foe on their side or rear. It assumes the foe will be preoccupied with the immediate threat in front of them while opportunity is sought to create another threat from an unexpected direction. As we saw was the case with Alexander's frontal assaults, the success of this tactic is often based on deception.

"The battle of Cannae, fought in the summer of 216 BC, was Hannibal's masterpiece." according to Peter Connolly in *Warfare in the Ancient World.* The Carthaginian commander Hannibal, the brilliant tactician, never lost a major battle in the many years he spent in Italy trying to overthrow the Roman republic. Hannibal had fought a major battle in each of the previous two years and the time had come for another. As the foes engaged one another outside the town of Cannae in Italy, Hannibal caused the troops in the middle of his line to subtly move backwards while the ends of his line held firm. Soon the opposing lines were conjoined in the shape of an arc when Hannibal called for the premeditated attack on each end of the Roman line. The soldiers on the edges of the Roman line faced with not only trying to force their will on the enemy in front of them, now encountered a new threat from their side, causing them to retreat towards the center. The Romans' ability to fight effectively was compromised by the multiple directions from which the enemy assailed them. Soon they were completely surrounded. Peter Connolly called it 'a black day' for the Romans.

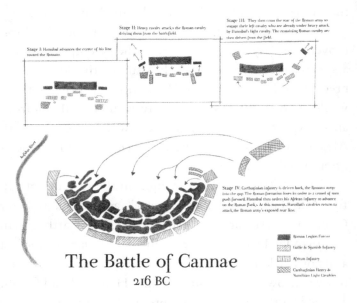

The Battle of Cannae
216 BC

As Admiral William H. McRaven said, in an interview at the Lyndon B. Johnson library, "turn the line and you'll win." We can recognize 'turning the line' as distracting a soldier with a new and unexpected threat. This distraction diminishes one's ability to face the task at hand.

Yes, satan (and the fallen) can do the same thing. As we have seen he is the father of lies, a master of deception. It is possible therefore, that some of the unexpected difficulties believers experience are satan's attempt at distracting God's people from their divinely appointed tasks. Lest we feel we're being overwhelmed by the enemy as the Romans were at Cannae, we'd do well to remember God's promise: "His grace is sufficient." In the direst of spiritual warfare this is always true. He is always enough. Because it's a fact about God, comfort from that promise doesn't even require faith, but simple recognition of who is our commander. Sometimes it's easier to rest in knowing who is God, than feeling faithful.

The **second object** in Clausewitz's dialogue on strategy, is to take possession of the enemy's materials and sources of strength. As we have seen God is above materialism, the only part of His creation that He desires is our hearts. Hence the very devotion of our heart is a battleground in spiritual warfare. Having previously defined the rebellious-to-God nature we possess as an enemy to our ability to live out our priesthood for God, it's easy to see this is a very heated battleground made up of conflicts that can't be avoided.

After Jesus's ascension, God began sending His Comforter on the day of Pentecost to all believers. While the associated gifts of empowerment may not be the same for everyone as what is recorded that first day the Holy Spirit came, it's clear that "In Him you also, when you heard the word of truth, the gospel of your salvation, and believed in him, were sealed with the promised Holy Spirit," *Eph 1:13*. God removed Himself from the physical dwelling of any given single place, namely the temple of the Jews. Instead since that first Pentecost after Jesus ascended, God has chosen to be represented by every single Christ follower through the physical presence of His Holy Spirit that literally takes residence with every single Christian. Not us, but Christ in us, becomes a source of the strength of God on earth, and in keeping with sound strategy, satan wants it.

Let's not give too much credit where it doesn't belong. Yes, satan was the original deceiver who lied to Adam and Eve, but it was their free-will decision that caused them to be removed from the garden where they lived with God. Since then it's clear that all of humanity inherited a nature like Adam, the intellectual and spiritual framework to be rebellious to God. "Therefore, just as sin came into the world through one man, and death through sin, and so death spread to all men because all sinned." *Rom 5:12*.

In *Christian Theology* Millard J. Erickson refers to mankind's capability, being unique among all of God's creatures, such that we can transform our experience on earth through memory, anticipation and imagination. Says Erickson, "This capability expands greatly, the possibilities of sinful action and/or thoughts." In the letter of James, the author describes how it happens, "But each person is tempted when he is lured and enticed by his own desire. Then desire when it has conceived gives birth to sin, and sin when it is fully grown brings forth death." *Jas 1:14-15*. Erickson suggests three fundamental forms of desire found in scripture: the desire to enjoy things, the desire to obtain things and the desire to achieve accomplishments. These all have roots in how God created us and so they can all be fulfilled in ways pleasing to God. Indeed, God will help in fulfilling these desires. However, through the inheritance we received from the first Adam, we all too easily corrupt these desires. The conception of such desires as James refers to, are those means of fulfillment that aren't in keeping with God's expectations for His people.

This is why, for example, it's never okay to compromise one's integrity to accomplish a great achievement. Considering that God isn't as concerned about our results, that is, He can do it himself if need be. He's more concerned about how we do it. "For the Lord God is a sun and shield; the Lord bestows favor and honor. No good thing does he withhold from those who walk uprightly." *Ps 84:11.* Here we see God is our sun (light, wisdom) and shield (spiritual & physical protector). While He gives favor and honor, He does so conditionally; to those whom He observes following His path. Note that it doesn't say He gives favor to those who get stuff done. All God's people have to do, to be blessed by their Savior is not be rebellious. To put all this in context, God gives wisdom and protection to those who try to follow Him and then He blesses them for their efforts. That's not to say finishing what God called us to do is irrelevant. To the contrary, God gave us the desire to achieve things, and remember, part of God's plan to guide our path is to impart contentment in whatever that path is. It must be mentioned here that often God's people misunderstand the goal of His plans because personal desires overrule obedience to their commander.

As an army confronts the enemy, the success of the engagement depends on the individual soldiers. One would expect simple discipline to be the requirement of success, but the very nature of self that we've defined as an enemy to our goal of following the Lord, adds much complexity to the experience.

Consider the Roman soldier. He's about to enter into conflict. He sees the enemy coming. He's not a machine. His mind is working as fast as his heart is beating. There are thoughts of bravado, perhaps overconfidence. There are fears of mortal frailty and maybe lack of confidence. Concerns of the opinion of others or even his own physical maladies impairing his ability to perform.

We can quantifiably define the experience of the individual soldier with the help of Jason J. Castillo in his book *Endurance and War*, thereby determining our expectations and informing an effective course of actions when fighting the enemy of our rebellious nature.

The foundational concern is the combat effectiveness of the individual, which Castillo says, is defined as their skill and will combined. Skill - how well an individual uses the weapons and tools they are given during conflict, is borne of the effectiveness of their training, to include the value of any helpful knowledge taught and physical preparedness to perform the required tasks. Will - how hard a soldier is willing to fight for the stated objectives amidst difficult circumstances.

The will of the soldier, which Castillo calls 'cohesion,' he defines as the individual and collective ability to "fight with determination and flexibility, while also resisting the internal pressure to collapse." This cohesion, Castillo says, is a dependent variable of two dimensions. A dependent variable in that the level of cohesion is constantly changing due to many inputs. In terms of spiritual warfare, we can see how our willingness to resist the rebellious desires of our nature is constantly changing depending on our surroundings and the scrutiny of our thoughts, not to mention the strength of our desires. The two dimensions are first, performance during conflict (fight with determination and flexibility) and second, staying power (resisting the internal pressure to collapse).

Castillo suggests a soldier's performance in this case, is not based so much on skill as it is determination, because possessing the right skills are no guarantee of effective performance in light of the variables aforementioned. If the proper skills are developed, then a determination to perform the necessary tasks is what leads to success. Determination is the motivation to continue to perform as trained with the intent to complete the objective.

Within spiritual warfare, determination can be seen as the result of faith in our commander the Lord. "Now faith is the assurance of things hoped for, the conviction of things not seen." *Heb 11:1*. Faith is explained by the author of Hebrews as the guarantee that our hoped for expectations will be met. It's important again here to remember that our expectations be defined by the Lord and not ourselves. Faith is also the proof of things we can't see, so it's obviously invaluable to us in spiritual warfare. Our commander can see the 'things' and He's guiding our path through the conflict of spiritual warfare. It's why, when we can't see the light at the end of the tunnel of our struggle, God guarantees the satisfactory conclusion will come, and His people can be determined to continue on His path.

The reason our faith can be a guarantee and proof is because it's not actually our faith, "For by grace you have been saved through faith. And this is not your own doing; it is the gift of God," *Eph 2:8.* Notice here "and this" *touto - that thing* is the faith that brings salvation in Christ, is itself a gift from God. It is, that thing, from God that is our proof and guarantee. That is the source of our determination as we fight that enemy - our rebellious nature. Since we know that faith itself is an endowment from God, according to Paul, it must be clearly understood that this determination is a result of faith not a byproduct of our choice to be faithful.

Castillo says it's possible to see evidence of determination, or in our case faith, which includes: defending when suddenly attacked, as opposed to fleeing from the struggle. Continuing to fight after suffering defeat, as opposed to giving up in exasperation after suffering loss. Carrying on in the face of prolonged bombardment, which is exactly how we describe the lengthy struggles we experience. Continuing to resist when surrounded by the enemy, as when we're in a spiritual battle in which we can see no way of escape.

Some further attributes, according to Castillo, of determined soldiers, or we can interject, faith-driven Christians are: "they maintain high levels of morale even when fighting." That is, they maintain a positive attitude while engaged in the struggle. As the author says in *James 1:2,* "Count it all joy, my brothers, when you meet trials of various kinds." This is because they understand the value of their efforts even if they can't comprehend the results.

Determined soldiers "will risk injury or death in order to perform their assigned missions." Although we read about believers suffering physical injury or death because of their proclaimed relationship with Jehovah, not very many who are reading this book are likely to experience it. That said, we should expect that God requires us to accept risk in the execution of our priesthood and subsequent spiritual warfare. Often the risk comes in ways the world doesn't perceive, being known only by the risk-taker and God himself. Consider the widow whom Jesus observed giving two mites. In today's terms these coins might be worth one dollar each. The nearby people seeing her giving this scant offering might have considered her stingy, but God knew better. Jesus knew it was all she had. She was willing to take great risk by giving what God compelled her to give. It must've been no small thing for her. She might have given in to the desire of obtaining things and kept at least one mite for herself. Instead she displayed a resolve of determination that originated in faith in God. In doing so she successfully fought the enemy of her sinful nature.

Further, Castillo says, "they prefer fighting to surrendering." Or in scriptural vernacular, "Blessed is the man who remains steadfast under trial, for when he has stood the test he will receive the crown of life, which God has promised to those who love him." *Jas 1:12.* So, although God supplies the strength, the equipment and the faith to persevere in spiritual warfare, He still wants to reward us just for our steadfastness on His behalf.

Flexibility is a further attribute of conflict performance, congruent with determination. "Flexibility describes the willingness of units to overcome panic when surprised or confronted with difficult conditions." The Roman soldier might often be surprised by unexpected events on the battlefield. These unexpected events might require unexpected or even unorthodox responses. The soldier's ability to adjust to conditions without diminishing performance is a result of their flexibility. He can operate this way because of his trust in the commander. With properly thorough discernment, the Christian might also consider their own surprise to unexpected spiritual warfare as unimportant because their Commander saw it coming and has a plan to redress the new situation. An aspect to spiritual warfare that is difficult for Christ followers to grasp in the midst of the struggle is that, while human limitations require knowledge and experience to come in linear form – one step after another, the Captain of the Host of the Lord sees all things concurrently in real time. Our Captain is never surprised by an enemy action.

The second dimension in Castillo's definition of cohesion is 'staying power.' To paraphrase Castillo in the context of our spiritual warfare, staying power is the willingness to continue to operate as planned when confronted with enemy pressure. For the Christ follower there is but one operational plan; to follow God, and this is usually with a perceived goal or end state in mind based on God's plans.

Further, enemy pressure is a good definition of the force behind the rebellious desires of human nature. Looking back on Paul's discourse in the letter to the

Romans in chapter 7, the impulses to do the things we know we don't want to do, sometimes feel like they have a power outside one's own will. This ought not come as a surprise. Jeremiah did remind us, "The heart is deceitful above all things, and desperately sick; who can understand it?" *Jer 17:9*. To be clear, our very own heart is *aqob - fraudulent, polluted*. Matthew Henry warns that "it is a common mistake among the children of men to think themselves, their own hearts at least, a great deal better than they really are." We want to be good. Therefore it's a simple deception to think ourselves better. But in Jeremiah's honest moment, he asks who can even comprehend how polluted our heart - our nature and consciousness, really is. Worse still Matthew Henry says, "this will be the aggravation of it, that they are self-deceivers, self-destroyers." We know we will not keep God's laws, particularly the chief laws as Jesus stated: to love God with all our heart and love others as ourselves. As the child becomes conscious of self interest and lies without being taught to, or takes their sibling's toy without being told to, our nature grows into more dominant exhibitions of self interest. The goal of our rebellious consciousness is the same thing as satan; to replace God as the chief author of our own destiny, to fulfill one's own desire without regard to anyone or anything else.

Even a person's desire to do good is often polluted by the self interest of pride. "Deceitful above all things." Meaning the most prominent aspect of every human being's nature is deceit. Not my words, God said it. And that is this enemy in spiritual warfare we're dealing with. God told Jeremiah that He searches the heart. If we know, then, that our very own nature can't be trusted, we'd do well to evaluate and question ourselves as we would with any other person we know that can't be trusted.

The goal of strong staying power is to remain effective agents of the commander, continued obedience to commands and overcoming internal dissension. To the Roman soldier this means maintaining an effective presence on the battlefield to outlast the strength of his opponent. To the Christian this means recognizing the sin process as it's transpiring. When the lure of rebellion to God presents itself, it can be recognized. Then before it conceives into sin, resistance to the lure should be engaged until the lure is abandoned by the enemy losing their staying power before us. That's spiritual warfare!

Its important to recognize that two mechanisms that erode staying power of a soldier, according to Castillo, are attrition and time. For the Roman soldier in the heat of confrontation with the enemy, to see a comrade fall is disconcerting, even as a casualty and not a fatality. The comrade's lack of presence is one less person to support the struggle. It's an all too close example of one's mortality or even just our frailty. If the comrade is someone cared for, then enter additional complex emotions of guilt, compassion and more.

Yes, the same is true for the Christian in spiritual warfare. When we see people around us fail it's equally disconcerting. If they fail or are struggling with the same problem, why should we even try? Better to avoid the problem altogether so as to avoid facing the discomfort of spiritual warfare. Avoiding discomfort is after all, one of the reasons we consent to the desires of self. Seeking the contentment of selfish desires is a false hope. It's obvious that the joy and peace of the Lord far surpasses anything we might hope to attain without God. Still, it's just easier to not fight.

Ultimately the Roman soldier has no idea why his comrade fell, whether it was his own mistake or the relentlessness of the enemy. Regardless of the reason, he's better off to continue fighting. He knows that, because he trusts his commander and he's been well trained to perform effectively with his weapons. But he still must resist the impulse to rebel against his commander's wishes by fleeing from the fight. The Roman legions did maintain the highest level of staying power because they believed their commander could accomplish his plans, either in the short term of winning the battle at hand, or the longer term policies for the kingdom. Does the believer in the midst of spiritual warfare know the Lord well enough to have complete and unwavering trust in their commander?

The ancient Greek commander Xenophon believed "I am sure that not numbers or strength bring victory in war, but whichever army goes into battle stronger in spirit, their enemies cannot withstand them."

Castillo's second recognizable mechanism that might erode staying power is time. There is the old idiom "idle hands are the devil's workshop." Military commanders of every age knew this to be true. Armies have proven to be mutinous. In the Roman Empire, legionnaires in garrison were kept busy with police work, road paving, building projects and guard duties.

Why this is so predictably true, can only be explained

by the 'deceitful above all things' nature of humanity. The human mind is capable of the most outrageously rebellious-to-God thoughts. It only takes time. Time to conceive the foolishness within oneself, combined with potential influence of the other enemies of God (satan or the influence of others around us). The compounding effect of mental treachery builds, the more time is allowed.

This exact same experience is realized by the person fighting spiritual warfare. It's easier to rejoice in a quick victory, than endure a longer protracted battle. It's easier for a parent to say "I'd die for my child" than to live their entire life fighting the spiritual warfare required to be a Christ-like parent for their child, or exemplary spouse or a friend for that matter. Sometimes God's people find themselves in a conflict that takes months or even years to conclude. Sometimes these longer battles are our own desires, conflicts or addictions. Sometimes they're with one of the other enemies of God, satan, members of our community or even family. And often in these extended conflicts of spiritual battle, time erodes our staying power and we get blindsided - outflanked - by our rebellious nature trying to flee from the battle in which God promised to help us through.

In these experiences, it's important to recognize situations as they develop, for what they are, thereby allowing the proper response. If we don't properly discern the circumstances, it's hard to fight the real battle that will bring victory.

Paul even alludes to this understanding of time being a friend of our foe. "Be angry and do not sin; do not let the sun go down on your anger, and give no opportunity to the devil." *Eph 4:26-27*. It's okay to be angry or offended by something, but the goal is to endure this experience with behavior that is pleasing to God. There are many selfish impulses our nature can conjure during these moments and it's a source of spiritual warfare to ensure they don't conceive. Paul says to not let too much time pass before we make an effort to resolve the issue. This isn't some arbitrary rule designed to force discipline on people. God gave this as a duty to those who would listen, for their own good. The more time passes, the potentially more difficult it will be to find a resolution, as the people involved will have a greater opportunity to conjure the mental gymnastics of deception that impair reconciliation. If we allow this to happen, Paul says we'll be giving opportunity to satan. (Or one of the other enemies of God).

Chuck Swindoll also alludes to the impact of time on our spiritual warfare in his book, *So, You Want To Be Like Christ?*. He offers the practical advice, to engage in the spiritual warfare of resisting these rebellious desires for a finite amount of time. This simple battle plan has a well perceived start and finish. It's easier to embrace this, than the idea that we must go on indefinitely with no hope in sight. Though we can't see the future, once engaged we can see what God will do.

The implied corollary, according to Castillo, to these definitions is that the probability of victory diminishes with the loss of staying power – to the point of retreat. The temptation of retreat for a soldier is the idea that it will relieve the suffering of the current conditions of conflict. That he will find peace after extricating himself from the battle.

This cannot be further from the truth and here's why. Clausewitz's eighth strategic principle is to "follow up our successes with the utmost energy. Only pursuit of the beaten enemy gives the fruits of victory." The reason for that is because the goal isn't to win a battle but to destroy the power of the enemy. The power of the enemy lies in the individual soldier and the easiest way to eliminate the individual is to accost them when they're least capable or willing to employ any resistance. The well trained or experienced soldier knows the perils of fleeing the conflict. This allows a pursuing enemy to maintain a position facing his foe with weapons at the ready to inflict harm, while one's own back is helplessly facing the enemy. A most dangerous posture indeed. In this situation the pursuing forces seek to inflict as much damage as possible while the resistance of the opposing forces are at its lowest ebb. When fleeing from the enemy, the hope of relief from the conflict usually never materializes. Worse still, the threat from the enemy remains while one's ability to resist diminishes when in flight.

We've established, the enemies of God seek to destroy His power so they can supplant His authority. There is no reason to expect we can peacefully walk away from spiritual warfare. Many Christ followers know this already, perhaps by trying. The idea that fleeing will bring relief, is a deception. One that makes God's people more vulnerable to the enemy.

As with the fundamental force behind 'staying power,' the main reason to resist the urge to flee is trust in the commander. Every good commander knows there are appropriate times to extricate his soldiers from conflict. They have methods of operation to retreat in an organized manner, that mitigates the risk of disengaging the enemy. Our greatest of commanders, the Lord of Hosts, knows full well when this is needed and will do so. "For everything there is a season, and a time for every matter under heaven" *Eccl 3:1*. As God gave King Solomon wisdom, He offers comfort in knowing the struggles we face in the pursuit of obedience to God, are seasonal. Our commander will always allow seasons of peace and healing amidst the spiritual warfare we confront.

The final **third object** in Clausewitz's dialogue on strategy is to gain public opinion. This recognizes the ability of a group of people, to force their collective will on others. In this case, there are combatants operating on behalf of a kingdom, and there is another group that finds cause to cease resistance to the enemy (which is in direct rebellion of the will of their ruler/commander who sees better than anyone, the hardships that would bring). If those seeking rebellious actions are great in number or are in advantageous positions in the community, the force of their will carries much weight in the affected society.

This has direct correlation in the believer's spiritual warfare; one of the enemies of God being others around us or as we established previously, society at large. It's helpful to understand how this enemy of God operates so as to recognize it when confronted by it. Then it's more easily possible to respond appropriately, but also to prepare accordingly before confronting this enemy.

Sometimes the effect of this enemy is seen by way of a political body, creating laws restricting believers from worshiping in a biblical model assembled with others of like faith. Sometimes this enemy works by way of unwritten social rules which gain strength when effectively positioned in the community. In either way, noncompliance is seen as bringing hardship and in some cases physical injury or even death. Compliance then, can bring personal peace at minimum, and possibly a greater acceptance within the community.

While some evolutions of a society's function don't need to be considered a threat, we have seen in places all over the world including our own community, that we're confronted with demands to conform to conduct and ideology that is in direct violation of the biblical worldview. Whether they come by way of laws threatening incarceration, or via rules that imply excommunication from good standing in the community for any non-compliant individuals, they leverage peer pressure to force a desired action or decision. Peer pressure isn't just for the teenage playground. It's found in any adult group setting. For example, in politics "you must vote for… or you're …" At work, "it's better for everyone if you…" In a church group, "you must follow… rules." Peer pressure wants actions without fruits of the Spirit of God. It wants consent to opinions that ignore our Creator. It encourages worship of false gods like materialism, fame or self.

It's important to remember that, while often conflict with this enemy includes direct interaction with individuals, Paul said it's not against flesh and blood that we fight. Therefore its helpful to focus our efforts against the ungodliness of the root cause of the issue at hand and not necessarily attempting to do harm to the individual whom God loves, whether they're a believer or not.

We must also see, that not every individual or group in society outside our Christian worldview should be treated as an enemy of YaHWeH. Clearly many we interact with don't present threats to our relationship with God. The follower of Christ should be ever cognizant of seeing Jesus as the perfect model of how to interact with others, It follows then, that any disagreement about worldview or doctrine or lifestyle shouldn't affect the Christ-like behavior of believers any more than it affected Jesus Himself.

Because societies are made up of individuals, and every one of them is fighting the same battles with a nature that's rebellious against God, we can predict conflict with others will look similar to that which we fight against our own nature. The narcissism, pride and deceit found in others is no different than that which we face internally.

These self-promoting qualities are the fruit of a common enemy we have with others. Fighting it in them, or in ourselves, is no different in that they inherited it the same as we did. We can separate the resulting conduct of the inherited nature from the individual, thereby contending with the consequences of human conduct instead of the person themselves, quite the same as we would while resisting our own private rebellions. It's pointless to hate oneself because of untoward desires, and beneficial instead, to despise the very desires themselves through increased appreciation of the grace and mercy of Christ. It is therefore possible to offer the love, compassion, grace and mercy of Christ to another person while simultaneously confronting the rebellion of the individual or collective rebellion of others.

There remains but one opinion for the believer's concern. That of the commander. The extent to which we consider someone else's opinion depends entirely on our valuation of that individual. To those we value higher, we give greater consideration of their opinion. Consider the toddler whose world revolves around the parent. The parent's opinion is singularly valuable to the child. Often a child will cry at the realization they offended the parent without any input of physical discipline. As the child grows older, they realize less dependency on the parent and other opinions begin to matter and compete with the parent's valuation in the mind of the child.

As the Christ follower seeks a condition of child-like faith in God, a similarly child-like dependence on God develops as a result, and with it greater valuation of God's opinion.

The ancient Roman historian Appian records an experience of one of Caesar's legions:

It was during the 1st century B.C. Roman civil war in which Julius Caesar sought to remove his political enemies by force of arms. His victory at the battle of Pharsalus, though it didn't conclude the fighting of the civil war, fatally broke the strength of his rival Pompey. In this, Caesar's famed 10th legion was instrumental. The renowned 10th legion was legendary for their courage and dedication to their commander. They saved the day in a battle against the Nervii tribes, and were chosen to participate in the invasion of Britain, as Caesar told in *The Gallic Wars.* When Caesar needed a bodyguard, they were his men. Having served Caesar for over 10 years, he addressed them as *"commilitones,"* fellow soldiers, indicating he considered them more than just tools at his disposal. They were proud to be addressed in such a familiar way by the one they revered and depended upon so much. And now they just helped him defeat the rich and powerful Pompey the Great.

But, even they fall prey to the worship of self. With their great benefactor having never let them down, suddenly they began to doubt Caesar's promises for their bonuses and retirement. They decided they would do no more. They decided to take matters into their own hands and mutinied with demands that he meet their requirements of discharge and bonuses. "Then Caesar came to them boldly standing in their midst," according to Appian, Caesar simply said, "I discharge you." Then, to their still greater astonishment, and while the silence was most profound, he added, "And I shall give you all that I have promised after I triumph with other soldiers." Caesar knew they had merely lost sight of trusting him, so he let them know he would not break his promises to them, but at the same time they understood his disappointment in them. Appian continues, "shame immediately took possession of all, and the consideration, mingled with jealousy, that while they would be thought to be abandoning their commander in the midst of so many enemies, others would join in the triumph instead of themselves, and they would lose the gains of the war in Africa, which were expected to be great, and become hateful to Caesar himself as well as to the opposite party.

Moved by these fears they remained still more silent and embarrassed, hoping that Caesar would yield and change his mind on account of his immediate necessity. But he remained silent also, until his friends urged him to say something more to them and not leave his old comrades of so many campaigns with a short and austere word." Then he began to speak, addressing them first as *quirites*, ordinary citizens, not *commilitones*, which implied that they were already discharged from the army and were private individuals. Appian says of them, "They could endure it no longer, but cried out that they repented of what they had done, and besought him to keep them in his service." Appian, *The Civil Wars*.

Their service to Caesar and the unimaginable deeds they accomplished, had become a source of pride, satisfaction and fulfillment to the men of the 10th legion, much like the experience of those seeking to follow the path of God. So much so that their selfish desires became subordinate to their will to serve him. They wanted Caesar more than money, and were willing to risk their life for that decision. This is a look at grown adults in the midst of a conflict between selfish desires, rebellious to their commander. The calmly honest chastisement of the words of their commander compelling them to see clearly that the fulfillment of their greatest desires rest in the service of their commander. This is what it looks like when mature Christians act on their conviction that God's is the most valued opinion of them.

An example of utilizing biblical wisdom to make sense of Paul's idea of spiritual warfare, shows how we can better understand our life with the Lord: "Lying lips are an abomination to the Lord, but those who act faithfully are his delight." *Prov 12:22.* Jehovah-Tsidkenu – God the righteous, is explaining to us that the deceitful behavior of His enemies is highly offensive to Him. If believers allow the enemy of self to act similarly to the other enemies of God, He is similarly offended by their behavior. Further, God delights in those who are successful in fighting spiritual warfare against the enemy of self, thus enabling that conduct which is indicative of the fruits of the Holy Spirit, and He therefore holds a high opinion of them.

Perhaps it's easier for the Christian to not hold God's opinion in such high esteem because we can't see Him physically or hear Him audibly. The more engaged one becomes in discovering who is the Lord of Hosts and what are His personal attributes, it becomes easier to see Him as Plutarch the Greek biographer described Pyrrhus, King of Epirus; "He directed the action as though he was watching it from a distance, yet He was everywhere himself, and always managed to be at hand to support his troops wherever the pressure was greatest."

Patterns of Conduct

Now that we've seen what it might look like to contend specifically with each of the enemies of God that are described in the Bible, there are general patterns that would be helpful to also mention here.

Looking back on some of the conduct of the enemies we face, there are patterns that form. Within these patterns, what might initially appear to be complex and insurmountable circumstances can with proper insight, be understood for their more shallow realities.

Deception. We've seen how Alexander's skirmishers were used to mask the movements of more powerful units. A form of active deception. We've seen Hannibal make unsuspected attacks to the sides of Roman formations, requiring premeditated plans of deception. We've heard Clausewitz instruct to never do what the enemy wants. Meaning one should always do what would surprise and deceive the enemy.

In warfare great efforts are made to use deception as a primary tool for success. This is because while the ability to force one's will on an opponent is always a hoped for possibility, it requires risk that is equal to the potential gain. By using deception, there is the possibility the opponent might make decisions or take actions that are exactly what one would desire, thereby minimizing the risk and making the gain more valuable. The opponent might avoid conflict or flee from it. They might surrender or become weakened and less capable of resisting a conflict.

In World War 2 the Allied Powers spent vast amounts of manpower and resources to create a 100% fake army. So thorough were their efforts that they officially assigned General Patton to lead it. The Germans regarded Patton as the most capable combat leader of all the allied commanders. The deception worked. The result was that key powerful units of the German army were delayed in reaching the Normandy beaches, resulting in weakened resistance met by the allied landings on D-Day. This is often regarded as a key element to the Allied victory of the Normandy invasion, thereby sealing conclusively the defeat of the Axis powers. That's the work of deception and its results.

We know that the heart of humanity is deceitful above all things, so much so that one cannot imagine the creativity and forcefulness of the depravity capable in the human consciousness. We see the corruption and conflict that arises from others and the world around us is an extension of that same rebellious-to-God human condition. We understand that satan, the being created by God, was the first rebel from God and the patriarch and creator of lies and deception. It's easy to realize that these enemies of God carry out spiritual warfare in the same way as mankind has been fighting wars for thousands of years; by using deceit as a primary tool.

There are at least 100 biblical verses about the concept, functions and warning of deception.

"Do not be deceived: God is not mocked, for whatever one sows, that will he also reap. *Gal 6:7*. Don't be deceived by the enemy of self.

"But be doers of the word, and not hearers only, deceiving yourselves." *Jas 1:22*. If one goes to the church building and hears a sermon and regularly reads the Bible, yet doesn't allow it to impact their behavior, they deceive themselves regarding their relationship with God.

"Beloved, do not believe every spirit, but test the spirits to see whether they are from God, for many false prophets have gone out into the world." *1 Jn 4:1*. Deception is a tool that others use to gain power and feel god-like.

"But the serpent said to the woman, 'You will not surely die'." *Gen 3:4*. All three of the enemies of God will not hesitate to offer misinformation that is a complete corruption of God's Word with absolutely no foundation in facts.

"And you will know the truth, and the truth will set you free." *Jn 8:32*. The wisdom and knowledge of God is the only apparatus capable of undermining the deception of the enemies.

If it's so predictable, why do people fall prey to deception so often? People often prefer to avoid the conflict that accompanies spiritual warfare. There are two possible reasons for this, according to Erin Leonard Ph.D. in an article on 09/12/22 for *Psychology Today*. The first is a matter of self-preservation. A desire to not experience the discomfort of the conflict or any potential unfavorable outcomes from it. The second reason is the possibility that the conflict may bring attention to one's own shortcomings. It's immediately obvious that both these reasons are grounded in the recalcitrant nature of the human condition. This, at the very least gives reason to scrutinize our motives before acting on them and at best, is justification to seek first the kingdom of God and His righteousness.

To the one who's operating in complete confidence of his commander; complete trust in the training and equipment from his commander and assurance in the commander's ability, there is no fear in the impending conflict. Overcoming the obstacles that block the path of the commander's plan is the best way to get where the commander wants us to be. That one finds these obstructions at hand on God's path is proof enough that what we're doing is beneficial to God and His kingdom, and us. Were it not, the enemies certainly wouldn't be wasting their energy.

Encirclement. This is another stratagem of the art of war. Consider the Jewish Sicarii Zealots in the mountaintop fortress of Masada. The Roman army came and built walls of circumvallation around the entire mountain of Masada to surround them. The goal of all that work was to cut them off from any communication with the rest of the world. It's understood that, according to Clausewitz, lines of communication with the commander, or with other soldiers who might offer help, are the lifeline of effectiveness for those who are engaged in conflict with the enemy. These lines of communication offer supplies of sustenance, equipment and guidance. The Jewish historian Josephus records that "hope deluded them" and, seeing no other way to avoid the desolation of the enemy's victory, the Jews committed suicide. All 960 men, women and children, with the exception of two women and five children.

The despair of hopelessness is all too common for those fighting spiritual warfare. Most people have a friend or family member that found that empty place of hopelessness where no victory or even escape was seemingly possible. It may be more obvious to others who see a person in this state, that God has the answers to their problem. Remembering that the primary device of God's enemies is deception, and how expertly they wield that tool, it's not surprising that some find themselves in this situation.

Christian or not, many people experience a prolonged struggle from many directions. The pain of loss, the temptation to worship other gods, and the compulsion to take charge of one's own destiny come in many forms and create very real pressure. As circumstances evolve, it's easy to lose sight of God. Losing focus on what's important in spiritual warfare is often caused by the friction of war.

Facing Adversity

Clausewitz dedicated a whole section in his book *Principles of War* to something he calls 'friction.' He resembles it to the friction created by the workings of an intricate machine. The difficulty "to remain faithful to the principles" caused by the complex uncertainties of conflict is the friction. While "complex uncertainties" is a good description of the life of many Christians, it's worth recognizing some of these causes of friction in spiritual warfare.

One of the causes is that we're often not as acquainted with the enemy as we assume. When confronted with resistance by one of God's enemies that we underestimated or even ignored, uneasiness is a natural outcome. From this uneasiness to indecision, then to poor judgment Clausewitz says are "scarcely discernible steps."

Another cause is the natural timidity of most people causing an exaggeration of perceived danger. Whether this is rooted in a safety mechanism with which God created us, or our self-centered nature to consider our own well being above all else, it's something that should be recognized.

Clausewitz also suggests that both overconfidence and self doubt can cause friction, stressing that the trust in one's ability to perform should be dependent upon training and preparation.

Insightfully, Clausewitz suggests on more than one occasion, that overcoming this friction is a matter of faith. Granted, the Christ follower maintains the object of faith rather differently than Clausewitz. We must be most careful in our focus of Christ–centered faith, and embrace that faith which the Lord has given us. Faith in Christ is the means to overcome indecisiveness in spiritual warfare. Faith is the means to overcome fear of an exaggerated danger of spiritual warfare. And faith in God's ability instead of what we can or can't do, is the means of recognizing His training and preparation are what will bring success in spiritual warfare.

Although it's not uncommon to 'feel' encircled by the enemy and completely cut off from any hope of help, it's never ever true. Ever... There is actually proof of this.

"Have I not commanded you? Be strong and courageous. Do not be frightened, and do not be dismayed, for the Lord your God is with you wherever you go." *Jos 1:9*. The Lord actually commanded Joshua to not be emotionally oppressed or physically incapacitated by the conflict. It's a directive. God said don't do it. The reason God would give such a command is because He also committed to be with us everywhere we go. Whether we're following God's path for us or not. Through whatever struggles we experience, self-inflicted or not. It's not just that He'll be with us, but, *yalak* - which implies God is supporting us along the way, not merely that He's at hand watching us.

Jesus himself said before He ascended to the Father

"look here now, I AM with you always, even unto the very end." *Mt 28:20 author's paraphrase.* As author Timothy Keller explains this fundamental aspect of God, "When Jesus Christ was in the garden of Gethsemane and the ultimate darkness was coming down on him and he knew it was coming, he didn't abandon you; he died for you. If Jesus Christ didn't abandon you in his darkness, the ultimate darkness, why would he abandon you now, in yours?" This is a commitment of the Lord Himself, not something we have any control over and not that we have any impact on. Though the evidence of this fact may differ depending on one's relationship with God, it's true for everyone who ever lived.

To consider that God has left us to our own devices is to deny God is who He said He is. It's a declaration that El Shaddai - the all sufficient One, is a God of broken promises. Even so, it's true that our spiritual vision or insight, says Paul in 1 Corinthians, resembles trying to look through a cloudy mirror. Between the onslaught of God's enemies and our own lack of insight, it's all too easy to not feel inspired by God's promise.

That being the case there is another proof. That is, what He's done in the past. God's past conduct is the physical proof of Immanuel - God with us, whom we can't actually see.

Recall in chapter two we talked about God instructing Moses to write a memorial of His help in defeating the Amalekites. God also instructed Moses to build a memorial of stones when the Jews crossed the Jordan river on dry ground. There are many other occurrences of God instructing memorials to be made, always so that recognition of God's help doesn't diminish with time. The Lord has worked for His people, and He has comforted His people in the past. Since the Lord never changes "Jesus Christ is the same yesterday and today and forever." *Heb 13:8* and never breaks His promises, then it's a matter of factual knowledge that He is always a supportive companion.

Forgetfulness is a human frailty. Forgetting is easy enough because our own nature is one of our enemies. Certainly then, remembering the things we see the Lord doing, is a God ordained tactic we can use to fight spiritual warfare. Are we considering ways to create memorials of God's work?

It must be remembered here, that 'The Way' of following Christ, is built within a Biblical construct of unity with other believers. While Immanuel is enough, often His help comes through the empowerment of others in one's life. Recalling the original prime directive from Jesus to love God completely and love others selflessly, Jesus then as we saw in chapter five, gave an additional directive. "To love one another: just as I have loved you, you also are to love one another." It's non-negotiable. It's a command. Love other believers as Jesus himself does each of us. That this requires an unnatural level of consideration for the church is indicated by the fact that it will be obvious to observers that the source of this ministration is Jesus Christ.

The Roman system illustrates that training together and participating in each others lives creates predictability in their dependence upon one another. Any single legionnaire didn't allow himself to be separated from his *commilitones* because there was safety in his proximity with them. Likewise he understood that his *commilitones* depended equally on his proximity to them. This system of codependence was implemented, supported and proven beforehand in peaceful times, when it was possible to help one another improve their abilities to serve the commander. So that by the time conflict was enjoined, there was no thought of question to the reliability of this codependence.

In Napoleon Buonaparte's book, *Military Maxims*, he makes it clear in maxims 26 & 97 that it's unsatisfactory to allow his forces to be divided by the enemy. We should similarly be cognizant of not allowing God's people to be divided by the enemy. We can safeguard God's kingdom against this threat in two ways.

Before we can articulate these details, let's recognize it's uncomfortable to be dependent upon anyone. Even humiliating. We want to be in control. That's our rebellious nature speaking. The biblical model of 'love one another' requires vulnerability. So just how serious are we about serving God? Are we willing to humble ourselves even enough to 'love one another?'

The first thing we can do to counter the threat of encirclement and division is seek those relationships which support us on our path of seeking God. The goal here is to find others of like faith, to build mutually beneficial regimens of training and support networks that can be trusted when spiritual warfare commences. We find our God ordained *contuburniums*.

Likewise and in the process of training and building support, the second thing to do, is to clearly present ourselves as one who is available to participate in our *commilitones* support networks and to actively encourage their 'God seeking' path.

Doing this will require different skills. In the Roman *contuburnium*, one soldier usually cooked for the others. Another soldier might maintain the leather work of their collective equipment. Yet another might tend to their pack animal. For the christian there are many gifts listed in the Bible. There are likely many not listed in the Bible too. It's possible that God might even utilize a skill or interest He blessed someone with before their salvation experience, and develop that into a valuable asset of His kingdom. Since Paul took several occasions to stress the value of one's skills to be used on God's behalf, it's important to realize what those skills are. This can only be discovered by seeking God and letting Him tutor us regarding His plans. To be sure though, it cannot be done by letting others teach us how to work miracles. Just like our participation in spiritual warfare, serving others is not about what we can do or want to do, but about what the Lord wants to do and what He can do.

One final principle worth mentioning is Napoleon's 7th maxim. "That the soldier should always have their arms and ammunition at hand" and "should be every day, every night and every hour, ready to offer all the resistance which it is capable of." To this end is why the Roman soldier trained with such earnest. To be ready, always.

Most of us have experienced the deceptive and swift onset of the enemies to create spiritual warfare of an intensity that can be shocking. For this reason it's advisable to be ready, always.

Paul told Timothy to "be ready in season and out of season" *2 Tim 4:2*. He wants us to be purposeful to make plans to serve God's people and fight spiritual warfare, and also to be prepared to do the same unexpectedly if the need arises.

Peter says to "in your hearts honor Christ the Lord as holy, always being prepared to make a defense to anyone who asks you for a reason for the hope that is in you" *1 Pet 3:15*. This could be a means of resistance against God's enemies, or it could be a means of serving the church. Either way this requires elements we previously mentioned; preparedness, training and obedience. In this passage, Peter is addressing the suffering nature of spiritual warfare, and that there is discomfort associated with it. Peter refers to Jesus Christ as the example of how to respond to the discomfort, or suffering. Correspondingly, if Christ is our model of conduct in spiritual warfare, then since He was vindicated through His suffering, so shall His people be.

Peter also instructs specifically regarding spiritual warfare, "Be sober-minded; be watchful." *1 Pet 5:8*. He wants us to be attentive to our spiritual health and thus being vigilant to respond appropriately towards God's enemies.

PART 2
The Armor Of God

CHAPTER 1

NOT YOUR ARMOR

"who is this uncircumcised Philistine, that he should defy the armies of the living God?"

1 Sam 17:26

Common Soldier   Optio   Centurian

Dr. Trevor Watkins refers to warfare as the "institutionalism of conflict." This conflict has been present since the garden gate was shut behind Adam and Eve, and since

127

then humanity has made a profession of it. So have God's enemies.

The materials of warfare evolved over time with the maturity of warfare itself. Early on, weapons were made of bone, wood or stone. Armor was fashioned from animal skins and later, fabrics like linen or wool. Eventually the science of metallurgy was applied to war and advances were made in the materials. Protective pieces were created to be more comfortable, effective and useful, and even look beautiful at the same time.

The use of a short spear was valued by lightly armored soldiers whose speed was their best skill. For them, having a thrusting weapon that projected farther than an enemy's sword was useful. Longer, heavier spears were used by heavily armored soldiers in dense formations. They could present their spear point to the enemy from several rows deep. Early Greek helmets were made of bronze and offered thorough protection. As conflict became more complex, requiring the use of auditory commands during battle, the helmet design had to be modified to allow ear hole cutouts so the soldiers could hear their commander's orders.

In the near east around ancient Israel, two different types of shield can be found in use. One, was a small round shield used by the lightly armored soldiers with small spears. This shield, perhaps 12 inches in diameter, is called a buckler and offered some small obstacle to parry the weapons of the enemy. The other shield was large and heavy with a curved top. Big enough to provide shelter for two people, it was usually managed by a shield-bearer who protected the combatants.

We see this in 1 Samuel 17. The Philistine soldier from Gath was so big he required his own shield-bearer. Goliath wore a brass helmet most likely conforming to the Philistine style, including a ring around the upper circumference of the helmet where decorative feathers were mounted. He wore scale armor which was basically a leather jacket with overlapping rows of small bronze plates attached to it. The inclusion, in Goliath's armor, of brass plates curved and shaped to cover his shins, called greaves, prompted Dr. Stager in *Biblical Archaeology Review* to suggest that these mysterious sea-people Philistines were descendants of the Mycenaean Greeks. Among his offensive tools, Goliath's spear bore an iron point that weighed perhaps 15 pounds.

After all the reviling and contempt Goliath offered to the host of the Lord, he was confronted by David, who "was but a youth, ruddy and handsome in appearance." *1 Sam 17:42.* In the fear filled Israelite camp, David's brothers got mad at him for speaking boldly in defiance of the Philistine champion. Attempting to divert attention from their own fear of the enemy champion, they even made accusations against David. After much persistence David was brought to King Saul. While offering weak examples of his qualification, it was clear that David wouldn't be deterred. He simply trusted God and any details about the encroaching danger would not dissuade him, whether they be bear claws, lion fangs or a 15 pound spear point.

King Saul then tried to give David his panoply of war gear that might at least be helpful in David's coming confrontation. This was no small gesture. Armor and weapons of any quality were rare in Israel. The Philistines in this period enjoyed a virtual monopoly on the availability of iron.

Upon considering how he would actually use the king's gear, he removed it and gave it back to Saul. He had not proven this gear in his own use. David wasn't familiar with it. He didn't have confidence in his ability to use Saul's battle gear to fight in what would be considered a conventional way. Clearly David had more confidence in what God could do, by just bringing what God had given him to the fight. Charles Swindoll, in a message at Dallas Theological Seminary chapel, said "you just can't wear someone else's armor." If David were to be successful in his battle against God's enemy, he had to use the tools God equipped him with.

Thus David approached his formidable foe, wearing only a tunic and sandals, and carrying his shepherd's staff along with his sling and a handful of stones from a nearby creek. It's one thing to talk about what one might do, but it's another thing to face an imposing enemy and being disparaged in a humiliating way in the presence of a large audience. David didn't overestimate his ability, or underestimate the enemy. He did properly esteem whatever preparation God had given him, along with what he could do with the empowerment of his Lord.

The heavily armed, and armored Goliath enjoyed a likely wingspan of nearly ten feet. His spear can be estimated at seven feet long. Further, his shield-bearer positioned the large shield a few paces in front of Goliath. Thus there would be no obvious weak points in Goliath's armor, and no realistic way to close ranks with him.

David had one tool at his disposal. One thing which God had given him. A sling, and the skill to use it.

Now this sling was no meager weapon. This is no 'Y' shaped piece of wood propelled by a rubber band. As much as three feet in length, these slings launch projectiles made of stone or even lead that have been found as big as tennis balls. The combination of missile size and velocity made them hard to see and defend against. They caused blunt force trauma so destructive as to shatter bones and damage organs even through armor, often with mortal results. According to Erich B. Anderson of *Warfare History Network*, "The most skilled slingers of the ancient world were even more accurate and had a far greater range than many archers, making them some of the most prized skirmishers available."

The sling's use was well known in biblical times. Judges chapter 20 and Chronicles chapter 12 both record the tribe of Benjamin as being highly skilled in the use of the sling. The Balearic Slingers were the most feared skirmishers in the Mediterranean Basin. Monopolizing the employment of them was incentive enough for the Romans to conquer the islands.

Facing Goliath, David had just the right tool. Faith. And the sling too. He didn't have to get too close to his foe, as Goliath would have expected. God had spent David's lifetime preparing him for this. All the training David had with the sling, and even his previous experiences of being in danger, led him to this point although he could never foresee it. David knew first hand what it felt like to be in a deadly situation, and what it looked like to see God provide the strength and wisdom to succeed. Those experiences with the bear and lion that seemingly had no relevance here were part of God's preparation for serving Him after all. God had it all planned.

We can see then, that the deadly nature of David's use of the sling wasn't so amazing. What was much more miraculous was David's willingness to engage this foe despite the uncertainty of all his peers. David sought the kingdom of God. Jehovah-Jireh guided his path, gave him the tools he needed and empowered him to perform. Up to this point, it's unlikely that David ever considered himself a warrior, and if he lost, his people would forfeit their sovereignty because of his failure. Yet here he was fighting the enemy army's champion in single combat in front of the eyes of the world.

In the first letter to the Corinthian church, Paul starts the letter by explaining that Jesus Christ is the wisdom and power of God. And to those called to be God's people he says to, "consider your calling, brothers: not many of you were wise according to worldly standards, not many were powerful, not many were of noble birth. But God chose what is foolish in the world to shame the wise; God chose what is weak in the world to shame the strong" *1 Cor 1:26-27*. When it comes to fighting God's enemies, a degree from a respected university won't help, nor will a lifelong commitment to martial arts. The power and wisdom of God found through Jesus Christ is the single requirement leading to success when fighting God's enemies just as it was for David in the encounter with his giant, and just as we'll see with the Armor of God.

It's easy to fill one's mind with images of all kinds of armor. With examples from the bronze age of Abrahams's time, all the way to the age of gunpowder, there is a vast catalog of designs and their usage to sample. In the Old Testament, the shield was used to describe God. He is our protector, by virtue of the fact that He is our healer, our Shepherd and all sufficient One. There were different types of swords used by the Egyptians, Greeks and Philistines. Some were steel, some bronze. Some were curved and others were straight. The imagery of a sword is used often to symbolize God's anger. Then again, sometimes it describes the power of Israel's enemies. Its intent was to summon thoughts of conflict, either on God's behalf or against His people. Armor was as diverse as the cultures we read about in the Old Testament. In some places in scripture it's described as a source of strength for those in power. And that's certainly how Paul is intending to portray the armor of God to the New Testament believer; as a source and symbol of strength for those who wear it.

CHAPTER 2

"TO THE FAITHFUL IN CHRIST"

"ON THIS ROCK"

In the letter to the church in Ephesus, Paul unfolds his imagery of the armor of God. It's a visual construct to help the believers better understand how the Lord is more than a savior who offers eternal security, by explaining how God does not then abandon His people to their own devices in a world full of evil. In an effort to better understand the armor and warfare illustration in the context of the letter's general purpose, we should observe some of the instructions he gives the church prior to mentioning the armor. This letter incorporates many spiritual truths which we looked at in Part One, so we can see how they graft together in the application of actually using the tools (armor) God gave us.

The letter to Ephesus is a wealth of knowledge and wisdom worthy of it's own study, but we can confidently dissect it to extract that which helps us understand spiritual warfare and the armor of God, if we diligently hold fast to the intent and context of the letter.

Jesus' Church

The focal point of this letter is the church, and it's purpose in God's plan. Paul addresses "the saints who are in Ephesus, and are faithful in Christ Jesus." *Eph 1:1.* The following information is for all believers, but with a condition: specifically for those who are faithful in Christ. Paul uses the term "in Christ" 27 times in the letter, and as many as 164 times in total depending on which letters one attributes to Paul. He defines the term in a letter to Corinth, "if anyone is in Christ, he is a new creation. The old has passed away; behold, the new has come." *2 Cor 5:17.* Those in Christ are first, saints, *hagios - holy, blameless, separated.* This is due to the Holy Spirit having come upon them following their salvation experience. Since then they have become literally new creations in Christ and their old record of rebellion against God has passed away.

But Paul adds in his address to the Ephesians, the description of 'faithful'. So he is addressing those born-again believers who are committed to 'the way' of following God. John R.W. Stott, in an article for the C.S. Lewis Institute, describes the faithful in Christ as follows, "These people have an inner serenity which adversity cannot disturb; it is the peace of Christ. They have a spiritual power that physical weakness cannot destroy; it is the power of Christ. They have a hidden vitality that even the process of dying and death cannot quench; it is the life of Christ." Here Stott is recognizing the tension of spiritual warfare, and the believer's ability to overcome it, or more correctly, the willingness of God to overcome it for us along with the impact it affords in the life of the faithful.

In the first parts of the letter to Ephesus, Paul discusses the nature of the church in Christ, and in the latter parts Paul instructs on the conduct of the church based on who we are in Christ. He addresses the expectation that the preferred conduct for those in Christ will lead to conflict between that which is of the world, and that which is in Christ. This chain of thought leads to the instruction of spiritual warfare and the armor of God in chapter six.

Dr. Thomas L. Constable in his, *Notes On Ephesians*, suggests this follows the teaching of Jesus to Peter "on this rock I will build my church, and the gates of hell shall not prevail against it." *Matt 16:18*. First Jesus declares Himself to be the foundation of the church. Christ, the builder will construct it, confirm, strengthen and embolden it. It is perhaps with this in mind that Peter later says in his first letter, "you yourselves like living stones are being built up as a spiritual house, to be a holy priesthood, to offer spiritual sacrifices acceptable to God through Jesus Christ." *1 Pet 2:5.* The church, or 'body politic,' as Matthew Henry calls it, is a spiritual household being built by Jesus Christ with living stones and for a reason. That is, to operate in their work for God which has been separated and reserved just for them. In this function of their priesthood they will offer 'spiritual sacrifices,' as opposed to the old way of offering physical sacrifices in the spiritually outdated temple building in Jerusalem. These spiritual sacrifices are offered by subordinating oneself to the will of God and include a consent to engage in the spiritual warfare that will always accompany the faithful.

The Lord then declares, although God's enemies will commence endless and ongoing attacks towards the church because of the nature of its foundation in Christ, that the gates of hell will not prevail in any way against the church. This phrase Jesus uses, 'the gates of hell,' creates specific imagery in the time of biblical writings that can be helpful to the believer. The walls and gates of an ancient city delineate the boundary of a secure space inside, from the rest of the world.

In the Roman world there is great distinction between the Roman Empire and the city of Rome. Although Rome controlled a vast empire of over 2 million square miles at its peak, the city of Rome was preserved as the singular point of governance. From there, the political will of power conveyed throughout the empire.

The walls and gates of Rome were seven miles in circumference. The city limits of Rome were called *the pomerium* and was clearly demarcated by evenly spaced white stones called *cippi*. Within and around these *cippi* were built the walls and gates. There was a sacred nature to the *pomerium* based on the desire to keep the seat of government and its functions pure. For this reason provincial governors or Roman generals were not allowed within for fear of the insincere or potentially rebellious motives of their influence. According to Philip Matyszak, in *Ancient Rome on Five Denarii A Day*, so serious was the sacred perception of the city boundary that a temple to the Roman goddess of war was built outside the city for generals seeking council with their deity, as well as temples to the other gods that didn't fit into the pantheon of Roman religion. The Roman senate even made accommodation to those senators serving as provincial governors which disallowed their entrance within the *pomerium*, by meeting on occasion outside city limits.

The construction of city gates was usually seen as an opportunity to display a society's enlightenment of artistic and architectural skills. They were formidable structures often displaying murals and reliefs that told stories of their heroic past. In a practical sense the walls and gates were the provision of safety for the city's inhabitants. In Rome's case, the city was sacked and looted in the early fourth century B.C., after which the defenses were bolstered such that no enemy army entered Rome again for 800 years! Even Hannibal of Carthage, although waging war on the Italian peninsula for over a decade while winning several major battles against Rome, surveyed the city walls and considered attacking the city to be a futile gesture.

It's important to note here for our illustration that by

the time of the New Testament writings, the majority of Roman citizens were not from Rome itself. Most were, like Paul, born somewhere else in the world and given by grace that which they couldn't attain themselves, citizenship to the kingdom. No matter where in the kingdom a citizen lived or visited, they were always connected to the seat and source of power in Rome itself by the vast network of Roman built roads. Any one of them could at any time solicit the attention of Roman governance as Paul did when he sought audience with Nero.

When Jesus used the description 'gates of hell,' He made a clear delineation between the kingdom of God and the influence of God's enemies. Like Rome and its empire, God possesses the universe as His creation, while He separates a space of security and governance within which the church exists, and from which God's will is introduced to the world. The gates of hell represent the boundary of the influence of evil, the termination point of the effective force behind the rebellion of all of God's enemies. It is this force that Jesus said will never prevail against His church. The reason this could be so, is that whenever a Christ-follower is in the midst of the conflict of spiritual warfare, they are never outside the secure space of governance of Jehovah-Nissi. So that even when a christian causes their own setbacks, it is still possible to possess the serenity, peace and vitality which adversity in spiritual warfare can't disturb nor death quench which Stott referred to.

Instructing on the nature of the church, Paul describes its eternal character. First he refers to the individual "even as He chose us in Him before the foundation of the world, that we should be holy and blameless before Him." *Eph 1:4*. He also instructs on the corporate plan of the eternal nature of the church, "and to bring to light for everyone what is the plan of the mystery hidden for ages in God, who created all things, so that through the church the manifold wisdom of God might now be made known to the rulers and authorities in the heavenly places." *Eph 3:9-10*. The idea of the church wasn't something Jesus just created in response to Peter's declaration of faith. Constable says, "The church is just as much a part of God's eternal plan for human history as the nation of Israel." God had it all planned from the beginning. In the progression of human history with God, He never revealed this part of His plans, so when it came to pass, it was a shocking surprise. That God would send His Holy Spirit in a way that Jews and gentiles could be commonly separated from the rebellious world was a new and unfathomable turn of events. It was in Paul's words, a mysterious revelation.

In Old Testament times, a gentile could become part of the household of Abraham by experiencing the proper physical modification to himself as outward proof to the world of his new station in life. This was a hint towards God's eventual plan following the resurrection of Christ, as New Testament believers similarly become spiritual heirs to the promise of Abraham by modification of the inner person.

We can understand this eternal nature of Christ's church in the context of the first part of God establishing our steps as we earlier read in chapter four, in that God had always planned for it. Further, the dual nature of the church as individual saints who Paul charges to be holy and blameless, and the unified body of Christ through whom God plans to display His diverse wisdom to the world, can be better visualized by our understanding of the Roman legions, and their reliance on the corporate well-being of the legion through the responsibility of the individual soldier.

Additionally Paul explains that the church is part of God's future plans. He describes in chapter 2 how the very nature of the church will display in the coming ages, the "immeasurable riches of his grace in kindness toward us in Christ Jesus." *vs7*, by virtue of the fact that though we "were dead in the trespasses and sins in which you once walked, following the course of this world, following the prince of the power of the air, the spirit that is now at work in the sons of disobedience – among whom we all once lived in the passions of our flesh, carrying out the desires of the body and the mind, and were by nature children of wrath, like the rest of mankind." vss *1-3*, God chose anyway to offer humanity grace and mercy through the redemption of Jesus Christ. "But God, being rich in mercy, because of the great love with which he loved us, even when we were dead in our trespasses, made us alive together with Christ." *vss 4-5*. Notice in *vss 1-3* that Paul mentions all three of the enemies that we previously identified in chapter 7. Yet the state of our being 'in Christ' exists regardless of our past or present contact with those enemies.

We can see then, the reason for the church's role in God's future plans is because our relationship with God is unique to His creation. The rest of the creatures on earth rely on the instincts God gave them for survival and have been given no expectation of an eternal existence. Nor can the angels experience a relationship with God like that which His people can enjoy. Some of the angels live committed to a position of eternal servitude and worship without ever experiencing redemption through Christ or an invitation to the marriage supper with the Lamb of God being dressed in fine linen. ["Hallelujah! For the Lord our God the Almighty reigns. Let us rejoice and exult and give him the glory, for the marriage of the Lamb has come, and his Bride has made herself ready; it was granted her to clothe herself with fine linen, bright and pure" – for the fine linen is the righteous deeds of the saints. And the angel said to me, "Write this: Blessed are those who are invited to the marriage supper of the Lamb."] *Rev 19:6-9.* Others of the angels chose to live in a state of rebellion against God. This is a similar condition into which humanity is born, the difference being that the angels were never offered even the opportunity to receive the grace and mercy of the Lord Jesus Christ. Thus it is the singular blessing of God's people to reflect the immeasurable riches of His grace in kindness.

Life in the Church

Given the incredible state of the existence of the believer, and perhaps because of the state of the enemies of God, Paul asks God's people to be those faithful ones. As it says in the KJV, "walk worthy of the vocation wherewith ye have been called." vs *4:1.*

Dr. Constable states that "the church cooperates with

God as He builds it." This cooperation can be summarized in chapter four first by the fundamental importance of the unity of individual believers with the corporate body of Christ. Being "with all humility and gentleness, with patience, bearing with one another in love, eager to maintain the unity of the Spirit in the bond of peace." vs *4:3*. This is based on a depth of consideration for others that is not only abnormal to the rebellious nature of humanity, but it's executed only by the supernatural power of the Holy Spirit.

This consideration of others manifests itself in the submission to others as a by-product of our submission to God, as Paul says, "submitting to one another out of reverence for Christ." vs *5:21*. This is not the wearing of a yoke like a beast of burden in the ownership of others, but as Paul has described, in humility, gentleness and patience forbearing one another in the love of Christ. Jesus Christ is the example for this submission. "Father, if you are willing, remove this cup from me. Nevertheless, not my will, but yours, be done." *Lk 22:42*. Had there been any other way than the path laid out before Him, Jesus might have preferred to take it, as He made clear while speaking to His Father. Understanding that there was no other way, Jesus subordinated His desires to the needs of others, to the extent of physical pain and emotional humiliation that He foresaw coming. With that example, there really is no justification for any self righteous reluctance of a Christ-follower against subordinating their desires to the needs of others.

Another way the body of Christ cooperates with God in building the church, is by manifesting the conduct 'worthy of their vocation.' Warren Wiersbe stated "The

Bible was written to be obeyed, and not simply studied, and this is why the words 'therefore' and 'wherefore' are repeated so often in the second half of Ephesians." Here Paul elaborates on what both proper and unacceptable conduct looks like for the christian. There are several of these behavioral lists which Martin Luther referred to as *haustafel - house rules*, in the new testament letters. They are helpful in making clear what are the expectations of God. Here again the execution of this behavior can only come by divine empowerment.

In chapter 1:18-19, Paul describes how he prays that believers would recognize the riches of God's blessings, and also that they would comprehend what God is capable of as He assists His people in their priesthood walk of seeking God first and His kingdom. The power of God being attendant to His people, is a persistent theme in the letter to Ephesus. Paul explains that this power from God is established by Christ's ability to orchestrate the eternal security of His people.

Paul confesses in verse 3:7 that even his ability to administer the wisdom of God is only by the operational strength of the power of God.

In Paul's closing prayer of chapter three, he expresses a desire that believers be "strengthened with power through His Spirit" *vs 16*. The purpose for the strength from God, unexpectedly, isn't merely to execute the *haustafel*, but to function wholly in the discharge of the fruits of the Spirit. "so that Christ may dwell in your hearts through faith – that you, being rooted and grounded in love, may have strength to comprehend with all the saints what is the breadth and length and height and depth, and to know the love of Christ that surpasses knowledge, that you may be filled with all the fullness of God." *vss 17-19*. In this regard, the power of God to positively impact our lives is literally unimaginable, "Now to him who is able to do far more abundantly than all that we ask or think, according to the power at work within us" *vs 20*.

Thus armed with appreciation for the blessed nature of the church and the empowerment of God to demonstrate the fruits of the spirit, believers can then address the issue of the lists. Respect of these lists is a matter of development for the believer. "speaking the truth in love, we are to grow up in every way into him who is the head, into Christ" *Eph 4:1*. This process is nothing less than the growing appreciation of a relationship with the Lord by experiencing God's power in the life of the believer.

The lists are a point of contact of spiritual warfare. As the enemy sends out skirmishers to discover weaknesses in his opponent, these points of contact are either met with strength and diminished in their impact on the combatant, or they reveal a source of frailty that will be exploited by the enemy. Now recognizing and implementing the principles of spiritual warfare as we previously discussed becomes important.

It's easy to recognize, often with the hindsight of lamentable experience, that spiritual warfare isn't won with physical tools or weapons. Human reasoning, secular philosophy or implements of destruction don't work because they don't address the root of the problems existent in spiritual warfare. Given the deceptive nature of the enemy's strategies, Paul cautions in the midst of his lists, to be ever vigilant in seeking God's wisdom. "Look carefully then how you walk, not as unwise but as wise, making the best use of the time, because the days are evil. Therefore do not be foolish, but understand what the will of the Lord is." *Eph 5:15-17.* Consider the foolishness of not availing oneself to all the accommodation that our commander has made on our behalf to guarantee our success in spiritual warfare. The time occupied by one's priesthood, God has planned to benefit His kingdom. The risk exists that any given day might become useless to God because of the rebellion against God that is present every day. Paul cautions that we should attempt to rescue every day from the risk of that day becoming useless to God.

Christians tend to exaggerate an increase of the presence of evil in their days of experience, but the days have literally been evil since Adam and Eve donned the fig leaves and walked away from God. The same evil and the same enemies of God have been present since then.

Because of this reality, Paul advises, "And do not get drunk with wine, for that is debauchery, but be filled with the Spirit, addressing one another in psalms and hymns and spiritual songs, singing and making melody to the Lord with your heart, giving thanks always and for everything to God the Father in the name of our Lord Jesus Christ," *vss 5:18-20*. While God has been sharing His displeasure with drunken debauchery for thousands of years as seen in the Psalms, Paul's message here is that if Christ-followers are going to be wise in their strategies of engagement against the evil, they should be singularly focused on who is God in the world and in their lives; by recognizing that our commander in spiritual warfare is the Alpha and Omega of our lives. The by-products of this recognition; the acclamation of God's blessing, the thankfulness, and the devotion towards the Lord, lead to the empowerment of the Holy Spirit.

And all this comes in the middle of the *haustafel*, in the midst of contact with the enemy.

Now - now we're ready to see how to use the armor of God!

CHAPTER 3

"FINALLY, BE STRONG IN THE LORD"

Paul has reminded the Ephesian believers who they are in 'Christ,' and articulated who the church is in Christ. He spoke of the necessity of spiritual warfare and what it looks like to be a faithful one.

Matthew Henry says here that it remains now for the christian to embrace the work and duty of believers. That will require one to "be both stout-hearted and well armed."

At the end of the *haustafel*, at the conclusion of explaining what right looks like, he advises how to execute those instructions. "Finally, be strong in the Lord and in the strength of his might." *Eph 6:10.* Finally... Moving forward henceforth, and above all things... Siblings 'in Christ,' be strong in the Lord. It's not possible to be strong enough by ourselves to succeed in spiritual warfare, so "be strong in the Lord." *Endunamoo en kurios*, enable the strength to make oneself strong – from the place where exists – the Supreme Authority. We don't need to look far to find where that supreme authority is. It's the Holy Spirit, and He's here now.

Dr. Constable points out that there are, "Three different Greek words for power in this verse, translated here [strong,] [strength,] and [might,] all of which appear in 1:19, and remind us that all of the Lord's almighty power and strength is available to us in our spiritual warfare.

As we've seen in the previous chapter, enabling that supernatural strength is done by worshiping our Alpha and Omega. Don't worry, no need to swing from the chandeliers. Worship of Adonai can be public and corporate, or private and as unique as every believer. What's important to any worship of the Lord, is to follow the example of the crazy guy who wears camel skins for clothing and eats insects. John the Baptist said, "He must increase, but I must decrease." *Jn 3:30.* That's not always as easy as it sounds, but it's a sure way to invite God to take charge of the work or conflict at hand. The result of which will be to capitalize on the intensity of God's ability to endure and accomplish the required experience.

A New Set of Tools

The Christian's execution of decreasing so God can increase, isn't left to the sheer will power of the believer. Paul acquaints the church to new tools God has made available for His people to accomplish this monumental undertaking of subordinating the rebellious enemy of self. *Enduo panoplia theos,* "Put on the whole armor of God" *Eph 6:11.* These tools have actually been around for as long as the Son of God has been, but Jesus Christ the Messiah has simply refashioned them for use by the church. Paul says there is a complete set of gear that we should devote ourselves to and array ourselves with, in its entirety, without neglecting a single piece. It's easy to discover, often the hard way, that the armor of God doesn't work well if one piece is left off or removed, or ignored.

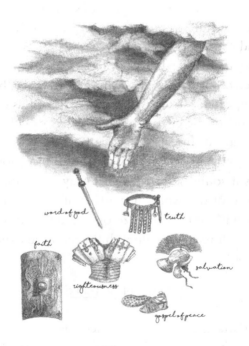

There is a requirement implied in verse 11 for the person engaged in spiritual warfare. That is to stand. To face the enemy, to square off with the opponent. The Roman soldier too, faced this singular goal. The Roman way to engage the enemy, as if to purposely set the example for Christians, was to march in a disciplined manner towards the enemy. Adrian Goldsworthy in *Roman Warfare,* describes how the noise of their war cries accompanied the banging of their swords against metallic edges of their shields in marching rhythm. At just the right moment they launched their javelins and then advanced hastily towards the enemy to take advantage of any disruption caused by their missiles. Often the enemy was advancing in a furious sprint towards them throwing caution to the wind. With a Roman display of self restraint, each individual soldier had to prepare to endure the impact of the enemy onslaught, absorbing the energy of their charge and standing their ground. Facing the enemy and standing firm in the midst of the fray meant also that they must recover from the offense of the enemy charge's initial impact and follow up with conduct fitting their responsibilities to the commander.

Dr. William Hendriksen of Calvin Theological Seminary, made the likeness in these words, "The 'standing' of which Paul speaks (verses 11, 14) is not that of a brick wall that is waiting passively, as it were, for the assault of the battering ram. The soldiers referred to here are drawn up in battle array and rushing into the fight. They are both defending themselves and attacking. Only when they make full use of God's armor will they be able to 'stand their ground,' that is, to withstand the foe, stand up against him, repulse his onrush and even gain ground ..."

Even though many may not be familiar with Roman warfare, this could be describing exactly one's experience in spiritual warfare. The attacks of God's enemies feel like they could physically knock you down. Yet those faithful must endure. Our commander expects us to endure, and this expectation isn't unjustified. He has given us His panoply of war equipment that is specifically suited to withstand the charges of the enemies and endure on to victory. More-so in the process of gaining victory we should remember that part of our commander's battle plan while guiding our path along the struggle, is to provide contentment along the way.

This armor is not only effective in creating the means to stand against the enemies, but Paul also specifies that it's a potent deterrent against their primary tactics; *methodeia* - trickery, to lie in wait, the ambushes and the deceptions of God's enemies.

Paul continues, to remind believers who the enemies are, because they're surely not who they seem. Dr. Constable observes that, "Probably the four terms used of our spiritual enemies in this verse do not identify four separate kinds of adversaries as much as they point out four characteristics of all of them."

Paul even instructs where the conflict will take place; "in heavenly places". We cannot assume this to mean that there is, or ever will be any conflict in the dwelling place of God because His kingdom is righteousness, peace and joy. *Rom 14:17*. Since that is a fact stated in God's word, it can never change nor are the enemies of God strong enough to force a change in that fact. There is also no biblical precedent for recognizing a heavenly realm below God's dwelling place and above the physical earthly realm. Therefore the remaining plausible explanation of this phrase is that, according to the NIV Application

Commentary, "it refers to the *reality* that encompasses life in relation to God, including both what God has given and what believers are called to do." Since our enemies are not corporeal, there is no geographical location for our battles. Therefore, Paul is indicating what is at risk to be gained or lost, which is the influence and benefaction of God in the modern world. More accurately, given the omnipotence of Elohim, it's the antithesis of that; what's actually at risk is the influence and malefaction of the enemies of God. Impacting the limit of their influence diminishes the long term consequences of their corruption.

It's helpful for commanders and soldiers alike to have some foreknowledge of the terrain of a potential battle site. Any geographical features of the local area might help gain advantage over the enemy if used correctly. Similarly for the believer, a fundamental recognition of the spiritual nature of our warfare and understanding the root spiritual cause of any particular conflict will help to gain advantage over the enemy. This is a failure point of many engaged in spiritual warfare; not recognizing the true nature and spiritual cause of a struggle. The result of this failure is that many tend to fight a false front of battle. It's a deception. In doing so we fight the enemy's flanking movement and even in prevailing there, won't win the battle. The strategically effective action is to find the source of enemy strength, the true cause of the conflict, and address it. Contend with it if need be. Display the fruits of the Spirit, stand on the principles of God's truth, and gain victory for the kingdom of God.

In verse 13 Paul reiterates the requirement to stand; to possess the staying power talked about previously, to outlast the enemy. He suggests that to do so, one must do everything they can; *katergazomai hapas* - ahead of time. Julius Caesar understood, by observing empirical evidence, that the success of his soldiers was facilitated by the instruction and training they received, well before any eminent conflict, and through the proper understanding of the experiences they previously participated in while following him. The evidence? It was that the quality of their performance directly paralleled the enthusiasm and extent of their preparation. The soldiers did everything possible to prepare for the next conflict.

Sadly, that isn't the case for many Christians. People tend to be reactionary instead of prepared. John R.W. Stott, who was in 2005 listed in the top 100 most influential people in the world warns, "A thorough knowledge of the enemy and a healthy respect for his prowess are a necessary preliminary to victory in war. Similarly, if we underestimate our spiritual enemy, we shall see no need for God's armor, we shall go out to the battle unarmed, with no weapons but our own puny strength, and we shall be quickly and ignominiously defeated."

With an understanding of the armor of God, one can prepare effectively to do everything possible to conduct themselves as the commander requires in spiritual warfare. Procedures for training will become more obvious as will strategies for one's conduct in spiritual warfare. The ability to properly cipher experiences we encounter as our commander is establishing our path, is also done with the use of His armor:

"My son, if you receive my words and treasure up my commandments with you, making your ear attentive to wisdom and inclining your heart to understanding; yes, if you call out for insight and raise your voice for understanding, if you seek it like silver and search for it as for hidden treasures, then you will understand the fear of the Lord and find the knowledge of God.

For the Lord gives wisdom; from his mouth come knowledge and understanding; he stores up sound wisdom for the upright; he is a shield to those who walk in integrity, guarding the paths of justice and watching over the way of his saints.

Then you will understand righteousness and justice and equity, every good path; for wisdom will come into your heart, and knowledge will be pleasant to your soul; discretion will watch over you, understanding will guard you, delivering you from the way of evil," *Pr 2:1-12*

So, having done all... Stand.

CHAPTER 4

THE BELT OF TRUTH

"Stand therefore, having fastened on the belt of truth,"

Eph 6:14.

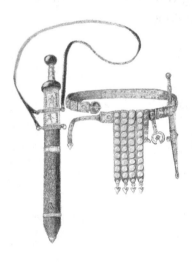

Paul mentions first, the belt of truth. The belt isn't the first piece of gear that a Roman soldier puts on, but it might be considered the chief cornerstone of the panoply of equipment. While it is important to embrace every tool in the arsenal, there are several pieces of the gear that just won't work without the belt. So what is the belt and its features, that caused Paul to liken it to truth as a tool to fight spiritual warfare?

The 'belt,' wasn't just a single strip of leather as one might imagine. It included a set of leather pieces of different sizes and functions. First there was the *balteus*, the horizontal belt buckled around the waist that helped hold the breastplate together. It was commonly adorned with plates of brass, copper or silver that were engraved and sometimes painted. This piece also served as a mounting point for the back-up weapon which was a dagger, called the *pugio*. From the front of this belt was a set of five or six vertical straps called the *cingulum*. These straps were likewise mounted with metal plates. These vertical straps added a visual and auditory element to the armor. The artistic detail and beauty of them were a means of individualizing the soldier's gear that reflected their wealth. Since their wealth was entirely indicative of their time in service and awards for outstanding service, the belts were a source of pride for the soldiers. Also, as the soldiers marched, the vertical belts swung side to side causing the plates to rattle in cadence to their march.

There was a leather baldric worn over the left shoulder and across the chest from which the sword hung. Then there was a leather strap attached to the inside of the shield with which the shield could be hung from the shoulder. There were others too, but one can already see how the panoply of equipment would be rendered useless without the set of belts.

Initially we can see truth as an indisputable value. Ultimately these are values set by YaHWeH. These values can be found in the original ten commandments as well as other statements by Jesus that instruct what are God's expectations. They are a reflection of our eternal Father. His very nature is the truth embodied in the values He has given us to define what is right and good, and what is wrong and bad. This encyclopedia of truth simultaneously defines the God whom we follow, and binds the *haustafel* which prescribe the borders of our behavior.

Truth You Can Wear

Since the armor of God represents tools with which we can fight spiritual warfare, there is another condition of truth to consider that has direct impact on our ability to confront the enemies of God.

This is the quality of being honest. It is the sincerity of mind and integrity of character. While the first definition is a simple recognition of what right looks like as defined by God, this understanding of truth requires a difficult response of behavior in keeping with God's expectations. Matthew Henry describes it as to "forsake evil, cleave to good."

"Behold, you delight in truth in the inward being, and you teach me wisdom in the secret heart." *Ps 51:6*. It's important to notice here that it's not the perfect execution of inward truth that is the subject, but the delight in the undertaking of it. The desire to seek it and the hope of attaining it is what signals God that one is trustworthy to receive His wisdom. This divine wisdom advises the path of behavior which is a reflection of Christ.

Peter, applying to followers of Christ the words of God given to the Israelites, said "but as he who called you is holy, you also be holy in all your conduct," *1Pet 1:15*. Holiness embodies the ideal of integrity of character in the likeness of Jesus Christ. Holiness is an attribute of the divine nature of God. It is one of His permanent qualities that can't be lost by Him. Millard J. Erickson describes, "Thus holiness is not an attribute of Adam, but it is of God. God's attributes are essential and inherent dimensions of His very nature."

Further, John Murray, in his article *Definitive Sanctification* in the Calvin Theological Journal April 1967, suggests, "The bearing of Jesus' death and resurrection upon our justification has been in the forefront of Protestant teaching. But their bearing upon sanctification has not been sufficiently appreciated." Yet the categorical result of this, Murray explains, is "justification is the foundation of sanctification in that it establishes the only proper relation on which a life of holiness can rest."

So then, it's not just the holiness of our character, but the holy character of Jesus, that is part of the armor of God. Since the Lord Jesus Christ is the perfect example of holiness, it then behooves the Christ follower to reproduce that same holiness in all our conduct. That's the belt of truth. When the believer puts that on, it's a tool to fight the enemies of God and find victory in spiritual warfare.

When Solomon said "The integrity of the upright guides them" *Prov 11:3,* we can understand that to mean that putting on the armor of God and reflecting the holiness of Christ will illuminate the victorious path through spiritual warfare.

What does this actually look like in the believer's daily walk in spiritual warfare? As we've seen, the fallen host may dress up like an angel of light and present deceptions for the Christian's choosing. Wearing the belt of truth of Christ's integrity will reveal the deception making it obvious as something to be avoided and illuminate the path of response,

The world may likewise offer lifestyles that lead down paths divergent to that which the Lord planned. Prioritizing the character of Christ might illuminate that the end of the path is nowhere God wants us.

Even one's selfish nature might be tempted to build altars to other gods. Using an honest reflection of the integrity of Christ will reveal any fraudulent deceptions in the mirror of one's heart.

In a practical sense, the outward appearance of living the holiness of Christ can be seen when one properly executes the *haustafel*. It may be an impossible task, but not if one is empowered with the wisdom of God that comes by a delight in truth. Watchman Nee advised of the need for God to maintain this piece of the armor of God, "no Christian can hope to enter the warfare of the ages [and to stand firm] without learning first to rest in Christ and in what He has done, and then, through the strength of the Holy Spirit within, to follow Him in a practical, holy life here on earth."

John Stott warns of the weak application of holiness in the life of the Christian. "Too much so-called 'holiness teaching' emphasizes a personal relationship to Jesus Christ without any attempt to indicate its consequences in terms of relationships with the people we live and work with. In contrast to such holiness-in-a-vacuum, which magnifies experiences and minimizes ethics, the apostles spelled out Christian duty in the concrete situations of everyday life and work." It's one thing to enjoy a worship experience, content in the sanctified nature of God's grace and mercy imparted to us, but it's something entirely different and much more difficult, to leave the safety of a group of friends and go out into the world feeding His sheep and reflecting the holiness of Christ."

It must be clarified here, because of the misunderstood term 'progressive sanctification' that the quality of one's holiness, or the success with which one reflects the holiness of Christ is entirely determined by decisions made by the believer. Still though, one doesn't fall short of the goal of reflecting Christ's holiness because they themselves are not 'holy enough' yet. To the contrary, as Tom Hall instructed during the Kerygma Ventures "Epic" conference of 2023, clearly articulating between the follower of Christ having experienced God's provision of rebirth into a new life with Christ thereby being decisively remade into something holy, and that which requires a continuous process of transformation into the likeness of Christ made possible by the permanent companionship of the Holy Spirit. He summarized, "I see it as both/and, that we are substantively set apart by God's claim that we belong to him. Then, as we continue to learn how 'belongers' live, we express practical holiness progressively."

John Murray describes this, "the saving action of each

person of the Godhead at the inception of the process of salvation insures the decisive character of the change thereby affected." Since, according to Millard J. Erickson, holiness is a dimension of God's moral purity, it is that which Jesus Christ exemplified while physically present on earth, and that same which God, in the intercourse of His plan, made accessible to believers by the Holy Spirit.

Holiness and Transformation

Paul teaches a resolute separation from the slavery to sin made possible by Christ's death and resurrection, and made manifest by one's baptism into Christ, "What shall we say then? Are we to continue in sin that grace may abound? By no means! How can we who died to sin still live in it? Do you not know that all of us who have been baptized into Christ Jesus were baptized into his death?" *Rom 6:1-4*. Murray describes this as "a definitive cleavage" from the old corruption to a calling of holiness.

Thus the inherent perfect holiness of God is present and accessible to every believer during every moment, and available to advise on every decision. By this God has conferred His holiness to us, having accomplished our sanctification through Jesus Christ. By God's grace and mercy one becomes immediately, 100 percent as sanctified as needed to gain access to heaven and be present with God, as well as instantly having access to all the holiness needed to fasten oneself with the belt of truth. Paul tells the Corinthian Christians, they "were washed, sanctified, and justified" *1 Cor. 6:11*. And Murray recognizes, "it is apparent that He coordinated their sanctification with effectual calling, with their identity as saints, with regeneration, and with justification."

It remains then, to conform the impulses of our old nature to our holy status before God, to better reflect the sanctity into which God has renewed us. This is the process Paul describes in the letter to the Roman Christians, "Do not be conformed to this world, but be transformed by the renewal of your mind, that by testing you may discern what is the will of God, what is good and acceptable and perfect." *Rom 12:2.* Paul instructs to discontinue the behavior of our lives before Christ and to make specific effort to seek the transformation of our desires to reflect the new nature that exists in us through the Holy Spirit.

We should recognize that this process of desiring to be transformed will not only instigate spiritual warfare by all the enemies of God, but will also facilitate our reflection of the holiness of Christ that will overcome the ensuing conflict. Pursuing this procedure of transformation will help to more reliably determine God's plan and expectations for us, but will also inform us as to what is that good, acceptable and perfect behavior that reflects the holiness of Christ.

We have noted how the belt(s) are essential for the use of other pieces of the armor. The belt holds the sword, not just keeping it in place but holding it up and supporting it. It also holds the breastplate in place, creating a boundary of movement for it. Without the belt, the breastplate would move freely, unpredictably and even unfavorably. Worn correctly, the breastplate works within the confines of the girdling of the belt.

The reason this is so predictably true, is because we're focusing on reproducing the integrity of Jesus and not the humanly flawed version of good character. Remembering that the most prominent quality of the human heart is deceit, including its depravity beyond comprehension, we should be vigilant to its impact on our integrity. Imagine sharing God's principles to a friend or coworker who recently saw you lying to your boss. It's not going to have the desired effect. It can't be stressed enough that the only way the armor works as advertised, is to use it as intended. Here that means being singularly fixated on a biblically based understanding of the integrity and character of Jesus Christ and imitating that.

Paul created helpful imagery in the words he chose for his instruction; *perizonnumi - to gird all around, that is, to fasten.* Gird, in English, is to encircle or bind, and to surround, enclose and hem-in. We are using verbiage indicative that a spiritual warfare strategy for the use of this piece of armor, is to plan on employing it to define boundaries and set parameters to our behavior. While we might expect our imitation of Jesus' character to release the power of God upon a situation, we can also envisage and indeed strive for it to bind and restrain the natural compulsion towards conduct unfit for priesthood and work of those who are seeking first the kingdom of God.

CHAPTER 5

THE BREASTPLATE OF RIGHTEOUSNESS

"Stand therefore... having on the breastplate of righteousness"

Eph 6:14 KJV

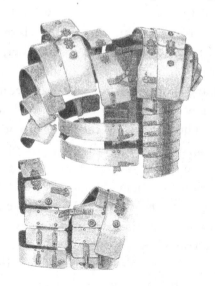

Having now a proper understanding of the belt and its usefulness, Paul says to invest oneself with the covering of the breastplate of righteousness.

The breastplate of the Roman soldier so familiar to people of the biblical Mediterranean world, might be rather unexpected to contemporary imagination. This is no single curved plate of bronze strapped to the torso. It's more a centipede-like collection of plates attached by internal leather strips and brass fittings, and covering the body front and back from shoulder to waist. The plate segments being overlapped, they become even more stacked upon themselves in the shoulder sections of this breastplate which is worn much like a jacket.

We call it *lorica segmentata*. This being a latin description of the armor, it's not clear what the men using it called it. Due to the design and construction, the large and strong plates allowed articulated movement while being difficult to separate from one another. This allowed hitherto unheard of range of movement for the user, particularly given the thorough security it provided. Considering the contemporary alternatives for protective equipment, the 15lb weight was a welcome technological advancement for its users. The thickness of the plates provided sufficient protection against almost all weapons of the ancient battlefield whether of cutting or thrusting type. Further, given the height advantage of many Roman enemies, the overlapping assemblage of the shoulder sections offered reliable immunity to the powerful downward slashes of the frenzied tribesmen.

The *segmentata* was comfortable, durable and preeminently capable of safeguarding its user. This author, along with associates of the experimental archaeology community, have gone so far as to pursue weaknesses in the armor while being worn, that might be exploited by the enemy on the battlefield. There are none. Though there are a few types of *lorica segmentata* known to have been used, as the technology advanced during it's nearly two centuries of use, it remained consummately capable of protecting the vital areas of the Roman soldier in battle.

Morally Justifiable Behavior

This is the equipment Paul likened to righteousness. Righteousness is liberally sprinkled in the dialogue of Christian circles, but what is it? Essentially, righteousness is morally justifiable action, and it's another of what Erickson describes as God's morally pure attributes. God is righteous. This is so because as Creator; "All things were made through him, and without him was not any thing made that was made." *Jn 1:3*, YaHWeH has prescribed what is morally just as exemplified by His nature. Thus God has subsequently defined what is unrighteous due to any misalignment with His morally pure nature.

In describing the armor of God, Paul is defining some actionable endeavor that emulates this expression of God's nature. There are many spiritual disciplines and religious duties one might perform to display morally justifiable action, which, given the corruptibility of the human heart and the nature of spiritual warfare, can be called to question.

Jesus himself identified for us, an unquestionable means to execute behavior that is morally justifiable. "seek first the kingdom of God and His righteousness" *Mt 6:33*. This statement by Jesus continues to be an integral part of spiritual warfare and the armor of God, so that the faithful should be giving it great consideration. If gaining an understanding of God's righteousness is the goal, Jesus states that seeking His kingdom is the means of reaching it.

Seeing Jesus execute this aspect of God's nature while in human form, the definitive aspect of Christ's behavior is His faithfulness to God's will. "Nevertheless, not my will, but yours, be done." *Lk 22:42*. This exemplified a steadfast pursuit of God's plan regardless of any divergent personal interests. It's the ultimate expression of seeking first the kingdom of God.

To see this further in action, one need look no further than Abraham. When God divulged His plan for the patriarch, Abraham agreed, believed and consented to the will of God. For this pursuit of God, it was "counted it to him as righteousness." *Gen 15:6*. So then, righteousness of God can be found in the uncomplicated attendance to God's will for the believer.

Job, like Paul, understood righteousness to be an action which covers oneself. "I put on righteousness, and it clothed me" *Job 29:14*. Clothing being a protection for the body, Paul makes the value of righteousness more impactful, likening it to steel armor. Inevitably Job recognizes the source of this protective righteousness, "I will get my knowledge from afar and ascribe righteousness to my Maker." *Job 36:3*.

Not coincidentally, pursuit of God's will is the only endeavor from which subsequent action or behavior might be morally justifiable. That is not to say all action or behavior is justifiable if done in the proclaimed pursuit of God. Creation cannot prescribe moral purity to anything they choose if it is aberrant to the nature of God or to the example of Jesus Christ. To identify righteousness in others, or in any attempt one might make to duplicate righteousness themselves, the example of Christ is the only benchmark for real morally justifiable action.

The Christian's discharge of the Jesus prototype to seek God, is their breastplate of righteousness. It is the actionable endeavor that will facilitate victory in spiritual warfare. Specifically, the genuine unpolished pursuit of the kingdom of God and His righteousness will produce behavior that will be defensible to the spiritually vital areas of the person engaged in spiritual warfare. As the *lorica segmentata* protects the beating heart, so does the righteousness of Christ, employed by the believer, protect the spiritual heart.

The Heart of Humanity

What then, is the breastplate of righteousness protecting? The spiritual heart. Easton's Bible Dictionary describes it as "the center not only of spiritual activity, but of all the operations of human life," and also as "the seat of the conscience." The International Standard Bible Encyclopedia specifies the heart as "representing the man himself, it was considered to be the seat of the emotions and passions and appetites," and further expresses the "center of moral, spiritual, intellectual life. In particular the heart is the place in which the process of self-consciousness is carried out, in which the soul is at home with itself, and is conscious of all its doing and suffering as its own. Hence, it is that men of 'courage' are called 'men of the heart;' that the Lord is said to speak 'in his heart' *Gen 8:21*; that men 'know in their own heart' *Deut 8:5*; that 'no one considers in his heart' *Isa 44:19.*"

That we have a heart is a reflection of being made in the image of God. "he raised up David to be their king, of whom he testified and said, 'I have found in David the son of Jesse a man after my heart, who will do all my will.'" *Acts 13:22.* While the heart of God represents His perfect holiness, righteousness and justice, it's the human heart that Jeremiah describes as corrupted and which Ezekiel says God will replace in His people, "And I will give you a new heart, and a new spirit I will put within you." *Eze 36:26.* It's this heart that is purified and separated by God and for His good works. "But a Jew is one inwardly, and circumcision is a matter of the heart, by the Spirit, not by the letter. His praise is not from man but from God." *Rom 2:29.* It's this heart that can then find parity with the church, "Now the full number of those who believed were of one heart and soul, and no one said that any of the things that belonged to him was his own, but they had everything in common." *Acts 4:32,* and provide an access point for God's work, "and hope does not put us to shame, because God's love has been poured into our hearts through the Holy Spirit who has been given to us." *Rom 5:5.*

The healthy function and well being of the spiritual heart is important to success in spiritual warfare. "The heart of the wise makes his speech judicious and adds persuasiveness to his lips." *Prov 16:23.* Solomon teaches that the spiritual heart condition impacts the effectiveness of believers.

Jesus taught that the very words discharging from our mouth are reflective of our heart condition. "For out of the abundance of the heart the mouth speaks." *Mt 12:34b*.

It's the heart that can be either focused on seeking God, "Trust in the Lord with all your heart" *Prov 3:5*, or fixed on a path of rebellion, "But if you have bitter jealousy and selfish ambition in your hearts, do not boast and be false to the truth." *Jas 3:14*.

With the goal of having the heart attending where God wants it, the Lord instructs Samuel to avoid focusing on the physical nature of things and look instead at what God sees, "But the Lord said to Samuel, Do not look on his appearance or on the height of his stature, because I have rejected him. For the Lord sees not as man sees: man looks on the outward appearance, but the Lord looks on the heart." *1 Sam 16:7*.

And it's from there, looking at the heart that God will dispense His perfect justice, "I the Lord search the heart and test the mind, to give every man according to his ways, according to the fruit of his deeds." *Jer 17:10*.

Solomon instructs that the health of our spiritual heart is determined by how one manages an emotional experience. "A happy heart makes the face cheerful, but heartache crushes the spirit." *Prov 15:13*. "A cheerful heart is good medicine, but a crushed spirit dries up the bones." *Prov 17:22*. We should expect then, that a practical function of the breastplate of righteousness is to provide a kingdom of God type of joy and peace due to the unassailable protection that comes from Jehovah-Tsidkenu, God of my righteousness. Paul is instructing that duplicating the righteousness of Christ will be the foundation of incorruptibility from which one can find comfort and satisfaction in the confidence of one's actions in spiritual warfare.

The new heart God gives His people can even be used as a tool to fight spiritual warfare. "Since, then, you have been raised with Christ, set your hearts on things above, where Christ is, seated at the right hand of God." *Col 3:1.* Jesus even taught that the decisions we make and priorities we establish, have an impact on our spiritual heart condition, "For where your treasure is, there your heart will be also." *Mt 6:21.*

Consequently we can see how important it is to create strategies of behavior based on the righteousness of Christ that will result in improved emotional and spiritual health.

Not only is the path towards righteousness restorative, but it is, in fact, the path on which God leads us as He's establishing our way. "He restores my soul. He leads me in paths of righteousness for his name's sake." *Ps 23:3.* We should recognize then, as does the Lord, that He stands to gain from our employment of the breastplate of righteousness.

CHAPTER 6

SHOES OF PREPARATION

"and having shod your feet with the preparation of the gospel of peace"

Eph 6:15 NKJV

It's strange to the modern reader that Paul would include shoes with the panoply of Roman war equipment, but as we'll see, these shoes, *caligae - plural for caliga*, were an important part of the soldier's furnishings. An article on

UNRV.com suggests, "advancements in footwear played an often overlooked part in their [the Roman Empire's] eventual expansion."

These shoes are more of a boot-like sandal, consisting of a multi layer sole of rugged construction, and an upper section using a series of slotted soft leather strips tied together from the open toe to the lower shin above the ankle. The bottom sole was then studded with iron hobnails.

The design allowed them to be mass produced even with a high level of quality. Their construction even accommodated the difference between left and right foot. Providing a better fit, this was something very uncommon in the ancient world to that point.

Shoemakers were highly regarded craftsmen in the 1st century A.D. and usually the practice of their skills was quite lucrative. Some shoemakers, or Sutors, were employed by the state and traveled with the army to manufacture and repair soldiers' footwear, thus maintaining the highest level of reliability in this important piece of gear. The certainty of the required level of manufacture was so fixed that caligae shoeprints dating to the 1st century A.D. found in Israel were nearly identical to shoeprints of similar date found in Britain.

The open design of the sandal-like shoe was breathable in warm weather, and easily allowed the addition of socks of linen or wool, thus offering comfort for a wide span of temperature. When wool socks were used, comfort was maintained even in wet conditions. Yet the uppers still offered suitable protection in rough terrain.

The iron cleats were roughly 3/8" in diameter and

depth with a slightly flattened head. They provided traction on the cobbled roads that stretched across the empire and offered exceptional off-road performance particularly in energetic and stressful conditions. The sound of these steel spikes added dramatic effect to the cadence of the legion in motion. It was noted that the legions would sometimes march quietly towards the enemy so that their footfalls and swinging *cingulum* were a fearsome sound, given their composed discipline in the face of the enemy.

The combination of design, quality materials and skilled craftsmanship yielded a shoe that was comfortable enough to mitigate the health problems that plagued soldiers all the way up to the 20th century, like blisters and trench foot that both can lead to infectious complications. Given the size and diversity of the Roman Empire, the caligae offered satisfactory performance for a wide range of geographical and climatic conditions.

Indeed this author has proven the benefit of this technology. Through cold mud or dusty heat, whether duplicating hand-to-hand combat, or marching or standing still for long periods, the caligae have proven to be a comfortable and dependable companion.

These caligae were in Paul's mind when he instructed us to shod one's feet with the preparation of the Gospel. Although shoes aren't a weapon, they are a valuable tool to employ in spiritual warfare.

Paul here brings to our attention the Gospel, which he describes as consisting of peace. To understand Paul's message, consider the origins of the gospel concept. A gospel is a story of good news that includes something given, implying there is a donor and a recipient. In its personal form, it can be a reward or donation to a messenger of good news. In its community setting, it might be a sacrifice to a god because of some occasion that benefits society. We see its formal application predating the biblical writers by centuries.

That's not to suggest the gospel writers plagiarized an idea and embellished a mythical story on Jesus's behalf. Indeed the foundational truth of this principle dates back the original sin of mankind. First Jehovah-Jireh fashioned clothing from leaves to cover the nakedness of Adam and Eve. God thereby offered the good news that regardless of their rebellion, He will provide a gift that will supply the covering they needed as a result of their sin. Then there was the supplementary ram that God provided for Abraham's sacrifice. As God continued to reveal His plan to the world, there was good news that the first born could be safeguarded from death, but only through the sacrifice of an unblemished lamb whose blood must be applied to the doorway of the enslaved Jew's house. Before the final revelation of God's good news for humanity through the sacrificial gift of Jesus Christ, that very humanity had themselves plagiarized the truth and evolved it in many forms to disrespectful and belittling versions of what God intended to show His great love for mankind.

Through literary device, Paul is representing the Gospel as the story of good news, that God provided the sacrificial gift of His Son to the benefit of all mankind. That benefit being the potential for restoration of any individual person into fellowship with God following repentance from one's sinful nature.

Paul further ascribes to this Gospel, that it's a source and provision of peace to those who receive the gift. This is a provision of freedom from disquieting or oppressive thoughts or emotions and Jesus himself made it clear that He offers it to His followers. "Peace I leave with you; my peace I give to you. Not as the world gives do I give to you. Let not your hearts be troubled, neither let them be afraid." *Jn 14:27*. Jesus can foresee that they will have experiences that will cause trouble for them. So, as Matthew Henry explains, upon His departure Jesus bequeaths this legacy to those who "are qualified [by God] to receive it." Jesus is clear that this is no ritualistic social formality as in "peace be with you," but a genuine "tranquility of mind arising from a sense of our justification before God. It is the counterpart of our pardons, and the composure of our minds." as Henry describes.

Since justification and pardoning from Elohim – the all powerful Creator, is the source of the available tranquility, Jesus reminds His followers that there is nothing to be afraid of. 'Let not your hearts be troubled.' That same heart which can be a stumbling block to the pursuit of God, or a tool which benefits His kingdom. Don't allow it to succumb to the anxiety and fears that accompany spiritual warfare.

Jesus emphasized this later when instructing His followers, "I have said these things to you, that in me you may have peace. In the world you will have tribulation. But take heart; I have overcome the world." *Jn 16:33*. A practical value of His peace lies in its impact on our spiritual warfare. Christ-followers will have tribulation, *thlipsis - be pressured* [from the enemies of God], *afflicted with anguish* [by the temptation to rebel against God] *and burdened with persecution* [for faithfulness to God]: a fitting description to the daily experiences of those seeking the kingdom of God. These prolific enemies of God that propagandize their *thlipsis* are actually not capable of inflicting any real harm to God's people by virtue of the fact that Jesus has already overcome the world and His power to do so is imparted to His church through the Holy Spirit.

A Firm Foundation

This is the Gospel of peace to which Paul refers us. However this isn't Paul's piece of armor. It's the source of effectiveness for Paul's equipment but not the tool itself. The device of spiritual warfare fighting power, Paul instructs, is another actionable process which God's people employ to successfully oppose the enemies. It's the 'preparation,' which stems from the root word *hetoimazo - to make ready provisions of internal fitness*, of the Gospel of peace. According to Clarence L. Haynes Jr., co-founder of The Bible Study Club, a transliteral definition can be to develop "a firm footing; a strong foundation."

Here Paul is drawing attention to the training of Roman soldiers so familiar to citizens throughout the empire. The legion's commitment to attend to it and the rigor with which they implement it, is well known. This example of commitment and the energy to accomplish it are worthy of duplicating.

Among the various disciplines included in the regimen of spiritual warfare training, Paul says, is to pursue an ever better understanding of the Gospel of peace. One can spend a lifetime in this pursuit, and experience a lifetime of realizing an ever deeper appreciation for this Gospel. The need, the plan, the preparation, the execution and the results are rooted in the divine wisdom of Jehovah and can be understood in part with assistance from the Helper. "But the Helper, the Holy Spirit, whom the Father will send in my name, he will teach you all things and bring to your remembrance all that I have said to you." *Jn 14:26.*

It's this particular teaching from the Helper, the understanding of the Gospel of peace that Paul associates with the usefulness of caligae. Like the Gospel of peace, for all the comfort and usability of the caligae, Paul is bringing attention to their importance to spiritual warfare.

The caligae may allow a soldier to march fifty miles in a day, but it's their performance in battle that make them the tool of choice for the people who are obeying their commander's orders. It's their ability to keep the soldier from slipping or being knocked off balance when experiencing the forceful onslaught of the enemy, and the firm footing they provide when the soldier launches an offensive movement against his resolute opponent. The caligae are the solid platform from which the soldier operates when in battle, and the understanding of the Gospel of peace is the same type of solid foundation from which one can successfully function in spiritual warfare. The better comprehension which this Gospel has had on one's life, the more solid the foundation from which to wage spiritual warfare.

We can't imagine a Roman soldier marching towards the enemy and upon seeing them, stop to put on their caligae. Nor would we expect a soldier to operate in enemy territory only to attempt donning their caligae after being suddenly attacked. The pre-planned function of wearing the caligae is a function of the soldier's readiness for action at all times, particularly given the uncertainties of combat (and spiritual warfare).

This is an imperturbability within which one can exist, that allows the execution of proper behavior amidst the conflict of spiritual warfare, that derives from the reality of one's relationship with God. As Dane Ortlund teaches in an article for The Gospel Coalition called *Christianity, A Peace-Fueled Battle*, "the weapon with which we now wage war is our cross-bought peace. Christianity is peace-fueled battle. All struggling divorced from gospel peace is counterproductive, like struggling in quicksand."

CHAPTER 7

THE SHIELD OF FAITH

"In all circumstances take up the shield of faith, with which you can extinguish all the flaming darts of the evil one"

Eph 6:16

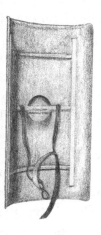

The shield. In Paul's Greek – *thureos- large door-shaped shield*. To the Romans – *scutum*. The ancient historian

Polybius wrote a detailed account of the Roman army, describing the *scutum* for us. It's constructed of layers of wood glued together, similar to modern plywood. Horizontally curved, it measures roughly 2.5 feet across and 4 feet high, and is covered with cloth and leather. There is a hole in the center of the shield across which the single grip handle is attached. Finally, a steel boss covers the handle hole called the *umbo* to protect the user's fist as it clenches the shield, and a ring of steel or brass covers the edges to ensure integrity against the slashing blows of enemy swords. It weighs roughly five pounds. Construction with the intent of lightening the shield was always scrutinized against the reality that a heavier shield was also more durable.

There were a wide variety of contemporary shields. The Celtic and Germanic tribes used hexagonal or oval shaped shields that were flat and often featured a central handle. The Greeks used a large round and dish-shaped shield with a forearm strap near the inside edge, and a grip handle at the opposing inside edge.

These all functioned differently than the *scutum* and we can see the use of these designs by their earlier counterparts in the Old Testament.

God told Abram, "I am thy shield" *Gen 15:1*

In the lyrics of one of David's songs, he says "But you, O Lord, are a shield about me" *Ps 3:3*.

Solomon instructs "He is a shield to those who take refuge in Him." *Prov 30:5b*.

God is a refuge and protection for His people and He creates this security through the teaching and comfort of the Holy Spirit and through the unified body of Christ.

True as this is, it's not what Paul is referring to as a piece of the armor of God. The Roman *scutum* is different from all the other shields. Some of them have some similar features and uses, but the aggregate of the Roman design offered functional gains exploited in the fighting techniques of the legionary soldier. Looking at these techniques will unlock the message behind Paul's illustration.

Michael Simkins in *Caesar's Legions*, illustrates a unique aspect of the *scutum's* usage, "The recruits would also be taught to use the legionary shield as a weapon as much as a defense. The boss of the shield was certainly used to punch opponents and the edge may have been used to strike an enemy in the face." From a fighting position, with the left foot a shoulder's breadth forward and offset from the back foot, the soldier would lift the front foot and lunge forward while raising the shield attempting to make contact with the *umbo* against the opponent's upper body. Thus unbalancing the enemy, the soldier having brought forward the rear foot, immediately lunges forward again this time to thrust upward with his sword before the opponent could regain composure. The Roman style was then a rhythm of parrying the shield and thrusting the sword that yielded domination over all enemies. As noted, in the melee of conflict, the metallic edges of the shield were also used aggressively, as the shape and balance of the *scutum* allowed a wide range of movement and function.

This author can attest to the effectiveness of the aggressive functions of the shield through the experimental reproduction of ancient combat.

The curved design of the *scutum* was useful in

deflecting the contact of the enemy's body or weapon without resulting in any unbalanced movement of the shield itself. If the soldier drew back his *scutum* closer to the body to repel an aggressive blow, the design allowed a quick transition toward an offensive lunge.

A common tactical use of the *scutum* design was to wet the leather covering of the shield before entering battle. This was done in anticipation of the frequent enemy stratagem of shooting flaming arrows at the legion. The reason arrows were employed this way is because they were generally ineffective against the legionary soldier. Roman armor being so thick and shields so sturdy, that the bolts either deflect away or prick harmlessly into the shield. Julius Caesar testified to this fact in his book *The Civil Wars*. He described the experience of one particularly obstinate centurion named Marcus Cassius Skaeva, who wouldn't yield his post to the enemy. "Skaeva, who lost an eye, was wounded in the hip and a shoulder, with a scutum pierced by arrows in one hundred and twenty different places, continued to hold the fortress gates of his jurisdiction." Thus to draw some advantage in the use of the bow and arrow, the enemies would wrap the forward shafts of the arrow with cloth soaked in some flammable substance like linseed oil or pitch, and light them before shooting.

The net gain in effectiveness of the arrows in this condition is zero. They are, in fact, no more dangerous than an arrow that's not 'flaming.' The Romans knew it, and the enemy knew it. The reason the enemy employed this strategy is as a form of psychological warfare. It's commonly understood that when one is presented with the sudden presence of fire too close to one's personal space, the natural response is anxiety and discomfort. The hoped for effect was an even brief distraction by which the enemy might gain advantage.

However, to the highly trained or well experienced Roman soldier, this occurrence is not problematic. Being focused on the truth about the arrows removes the need for their concern. Persevering on their intended course of action allowed the wet leather of the *scutum* to perform as expected and quench the flaming arrows.

Another tactical use of the shield was for a group of soldiers to form a *testudo* in which shields were held out front or overhead to create a tortoise-like visual and protective effect. While this might be seen as a defensive posture, it was primarily used to move forward in the face of an enemy barrage of missiles. Very seldom was there occasion for the Roman soldier to stand stationary hiding behind the shield. That was in no way part of the tactics around which the shield functioned.

This is the shield of faith. This is what Paul used to illustrate the faith of a believer. He says to utilize this tool *Epi pas - in all manner of situations*. With the same diversity of application the Roman soldier finds advantage with the *scutum*, in all manner of spiritual warfare, faith is beneficial for the Christ follower.

Commitment to God

Faith, in its simplicity, is fidelity, or strict observance to one's commitment. Dr. Constable explains that the operation of faith for the believer "is two-fold: First, it is trust in all that God has revealed, and second, it is the active application of that trust at the moment of spiritual attack." Understanding the aggressive nature of the *scutum's* usage, we can see that Paul is emphasizing the active application of faith to the benefit of the kingdom of God.

That humanity is capable of faith directed toward the triune Elohim, reflects first that our Creator was strictly observant to His promises to us. "Your steadfast love, O Lord, extends to the heavens, your faithfulness to the clouds." *Ps 36:5.* Specifically He is unwaveringly committed to helping humanity in ways that we can't help ourselves. "If we confess our sins, he is faithful and just to forgive us our sins and to cleanse us from all unrighteousness." *1Jn 1:9.* In this faithfulness we see God in a way that no other god can be described. "O Lord God of hosts, who is mighty as you are, O Lord, with your faithfulness all around you?" *Ps 89:8.* There is no one, nor anywhere else one might find the absolute ability to demonstrate perfect faithfulness toward someone. Friends can't do it. Family members can't do it. All the money in the world can't do it, nor can fame, power and influence. Only God.

The Lord desires to impart His attribute of faithfulness to anyone in His creation who is willing to embrace it, and He has a plan to communicate it through the Helper Holy Spirit. "So faith comes from hearing, and hearing through the word of Christ." *Rom 10:17.* By this the wise King Solomon considered that every morning one awakens, there is evidence of the beneficence of God's faithfulness. "The steadfast love of the Lord never ceases; his mercies never come to an end; they are new every morning; great is your faithfulness." *Lam 3:22&23.*

God described the faith-based relationship with Him to Hosea, "I will betroth you to me in faithfulness. And you shall know the Lord." *Hos 2:20.* This relationship with the Lord is conceived when God 'betroths' *araw (pronounced aw-ras) - espouse - that is, to adopt, embrace and make one's own*, someone into a new affiliation with Him that was previously impossible. In this, Todd Golden, pastor, missionary and U.S. Army Chaplain, describes faith from the Lord as "belief that possesses us, not that we possess."

Like God's faithfulness on our behalf, one's reciprocal faith directed toward Adonai, can be understood to exist by the demonstration of some kind of action. If God hadn't initiated activity to mankind's benefit, He wouldn't have been faithful. Likewise, the born–again believer expresses a new worldview that implies the expression of action to validate the belief. "If a brother or sister is poorly clothed and lacking in daily food, and one of you says to them, [Go in peace, be warmed and filled,] without giving them the things needed for the body, what good is that? So also faith by itself, if it does not have works, is dead." *Jas 2:15-17.* Not that actions, or works, are required to convince God to embrace the relationship, but like God, if one doesn't initiate some kind of action to express the new found relationship, then it's difficult to justify the legitimacy of the relationship. Far from being coercion to do stuff for God, it's that El Elyon the most high God was our faith example worthy to emulate. We use faith(ful) as a description of God or even exemplary believers, but this portrayal can exist only as the object of an expression of action. T. Golden instructs, "Faith isn't seen by what we say we believe. Faith is seen by our daily actions of trust."

Jesus instructed that faith manifests action, "Jesus answered them, 'Truly, I say to you, if you have faith and do not doubt, you will not only do what has been done to the fig tree, but even if you say to this mountain, 'Be taken up and thrown into the sea,' it will happen.'" *Mt 21:21.* He's describing action only possible through the empowerment of the Holy Spirit as a result of strict observance of one's commitment to God.

The writer of the Hebrews letter expresses the connection between the breastplate of righteousness and the shield of faith, "but my righteous one shall live by faith, and if he shrinks back, my soul has no pleasure in him." *Heb 10:38.* With Christ as our example, righteousness (steadfast pursuit of God's will) is implemented 'by faith' (strict observance of commitment to God). We must remember here that none of this is possible without input from the counselor and helper, the Holy Spirit. We can see in that verse also, faith – the object of action, contrasted against how God finds displeasure in one's action of withholding out of sight, cowering or shrinking or holding reservation to any required action in spiritual warfare. It's inferred by this that the expression of action that results from faith, is action that is beneficial to the kingdom of God; the proliferation of God's influence, and that this is what's pleasing to God. In fact, it is impossible to please God without this expression of action based on our professed commitment to Him, "And without faith it is impossible to please Him, for whoever would draw near to God must believe that he exists and that he rewards those who seek Him." *Heb 11:6.*

Looking further into God's value system, it's helpful to understand why His opinion is motivated by faith activity. "A faithful man will abound with blessings, but whoever hastens to be rich will not go unpunished." *Prov 28:20.* Getting to the root of Solomon's message, someone 'hastening to be rich,' suggests the efforts to help oneself, to prioritize self and to calculate one's well being above all else. Whether Christ-follower or not, this behavior will be recompensed with eternal implications according to God's perfect justice. Solomon's alternative is faithfulness to God, and this action will lead to the abundance of God's blessing. Jesus too offers insight into God's priority values; "Woe to you, scribes and Pharisees, hypocrites! For you tithe mint and dill and cumin, and have neglected the weightier matters of the law: justice and mercy and faithfulness." *Mt 23:23a*. Here the implication is that the hypocrites perform actions for their own self interest – even by way of tithing! – while neglecting God's principles of justice, mercy and faithfulness, which the Lord considers matters of greater importance.

The apostles asked Jesus to increase their faith. "The apostles said to the Lord, 'Increase our faith!' And the Lord said, If you had faith like a grain of mustard seed, you could say to this mulberry tree, 'Be uprooted and planted in the sea,' and it would obey you." *Lk 17:5-6*. They didn't need more faith, they needed to operate with power, the faith God imparted to them.

Jesus follows this in *vss 6-10* with additional considerations regarding faith. T. Golden explains that, here, the Lord used a parable to clarify that the empowerment of God that results in our faith actions isn't about our perception of our faith, but about Jesus being the sole object and source of the mountain–moving faith. Therefore nothing is impossible in our priesthood/seeking/ walking with God because nothing is impossible for God.

Further in these verses, He expects His followers to duplicate the observance of commitment which He is offering on our behalf. Jesus describes servants who follow the commands of their master: there is nothing noteworthy, Jesus says, about simply following orders. For the Christian, faith-based behavior is a matter of obedience to our commander in spiritual warfare. While not particularly meritorious conduct since God expects it, He is, however, pleased by it. Is this an unpleasant burden for the Christian to bear? Jesus spoke these words with the foreknowledge of His coming humiliation and suffering through which He would demonstrate His example of faithfulness. "looking to Jesus, the founder and perfecter of our faith, who for the joy that was set before him endured the cross, despising the shame, and is seated at the right hand of the throne of God." *Heb 12:2*. It is therefore justifiable that He expects the response of faith one might embrace, of the mountain moving empowerment He offers us, as we seek His kingdom.

Faith and the Christian life

Faith is part of a condition within which the believer lives. "So now faith, hope, and love abide, these three; but the greatest of these is love." *1Cor 13:13*. These three expressions of God will continue to exist in an immovable position of relevance to the Christian. Hope is our trust in God. Faith is our action response to that trust. And love is the governing doctrine of behavior within which the believer takes action on that hope and faith. Taken together this should oblige a rule of conduct which affects one's entire life. Suddenly one must ask themselves questions like "how does this decision (or desire) represent my strict observance of my commitment to God and faithfulness to Him?"

There are many corresponding effects from the exercise of faith in the life of the believer, and they all contribute to success in spiritual warfare.

Faith is the opposite of fear. "He said to them, Why are you so afraid? Have you still no faith?" *Mk 4:40*. When one operates in faith of the commander, there is no room for fear.

Faith purifies. "and he made no distinction between us and them, having cleansed their hearts by faith." *Acts 15:9.* Embracing the faith offered by God is the means by which the enemy of self and the personal burden of rebellion against God, is overcome. This itself is weaponized and becomes the shield used offensively to take ground for the kingdom of God.

Faith justifies. "Therefore, since we have been justified by faith, we have peace with God through our Lord Jesus Christ." *Rom 5:1.* Receiving faith from God offers access to the personal application of the Gospel of Jesus Christ, which as we have seen, offers peace and is also adopted to fight spiritual warfare.

Faith provides access to God's grace. "Through him we have also obtained access by faith into this grace in which we stand, and we rejoice in hope of the glory of God." *Rom 5:2.* It's this undeserved kindness from El-Shaddai, the all sufficient One, that generates contentment even in the midst of spiritual warfare.

Faith produces patience. "Count it all joy, my brothers, when you meet trials of various kinds, for you know that the testing of your faith produces steadfastness. And let steadfastness have its full effect, that you may be perfect and complete, lacking in nothing." *Jas 1:2-4.* Understanding the function of faith is helpful for the believer to succeed in spiritual warfare. James instructs that executing faith based actions in the heat of spiritual warfare (the testing of our faith), and the success one achieves by it, will encourage the believer to be more firmly grounded on their path of seeking the kingdom of God. This is a circularly fruitful endeavor. Faithfulness begets ever greater steadfastness, which makes it easier to be ever more strictly observant of one's commitment to God. This is why centurions taught new recruits, and why we seek the wise counsel of our church elders.

Faith unlocks God's wisdom. "By faith we understand that the universe was created by the word of God, so that what is seen was not made out of things that are visible." *Heb 11:3.* The revelation of God's wisdom, being a function of the Counselor Holy Spirit, we can understand this to indicate that faith based action of the believer will encourage increasing input from the Holy Spirit. When a soldier is executing the orders of his commander, the commander makes provision for the soldier's success.

Paul instructs that there is a unity of the life of faith for believers. "until we all attain to the unity of the faith and of the knowledge of the Son of God," *Eph 4:13a.* Indeed since faith action is the path to the true wisdom of God and incorruptible kingdom service, it's also the trusted path to find unity in the church. This is important since it's God's plan for every Christian to operate in their priesthood within the body of Christ. Like the use of the *scutum* in the tortoise formation, God plans for one's faith to be beneficial to the church as they are unified in the action of taking ground from the enemies.

Faith is a suitable substitute for self reliance. "for we walk by faith, not by sight." *2 Cor 5:7.* Many people try to fight spiritual warfare based on what they see of the physical world and based on the wisdom and insight of the world. It starts as a hopeful endeavor. It offers a sense of control and independence. When one brings their own tools to fight spiritual warfare, disappointment is imminent. However everyone must account for themselves to God. Some wait for the end of this life when it's too late. Those 'in Christ' have done so in this life by embracing the faith of Christ, and by this they embark on a new life based entirely on how they fit into the kingdom of God.

The Hebrews author defines faith as "Now faith is the assurance of things hoped for, the conviction of things not seen." *Heb 11:1*. When the spiritual truth of God and His promises are so strongly understood without any physical evidence, that they would be substantiated by the faith action of the believer, it is assurance and conviction to the world that the kingdom of God is at hand. As Keith Green said, that God could change someone's heart is a greater miracle than any divine subjugation of the laws of physics. This is why the supernatural love of God as seen by the world is the thing that will corroborate one's commitment to Christ. It's a faith based behavioral change that is obvious to the world.

This assurance and conviction is also the function of faith that performs like the wet leather of the *scutum*. The assaults of the enemies of God, like an ancient arrow shot, are ineffectual to the performance of God's people in spiritual warfare. The Christian soldier, like their Roman counterpart, sees the enemies engage in psychological warfare to make the assaults appear more harmful than they really are. To the well trained or experienced Christian, they too can perceive the actual harmlessness of these deceptions, and thus carry on with the commander's plan of action. The assurance and conviction associated with the faithful, forward moving action of the believer quenches the otherwise intimidating flames of the feeble deceptions of the enemy.

It can be observed then, that as the Roman soldier uses his shield offensively to expand the strength and influence of the empire, so does the believer utilize faith to the increase of God's strength and influence in the present world. So that the very act of standing 'firm in the faith' *1 Cor 16:13*, is a means of pleasing God by carrying out the action of resisting the aggressive activity of the enemies of God. Every faith based step one takes is like a lunge forward with the effect of an *umbo* pummeling God's enemies.

Faith is the tool that the apostle John says will bring victory in spiritual warfare. "For everyone who has been born of God overcomes the world. And this is the victory that has overcome the world—our faith. Who is it that overcomes the world except the one who believes that Jesus is the Son of God?" *1 Jn 5:4-5*.

CHAPTER 8

THE HELMET OF SALVATION

"Take the helmet of salvation"

Eph 6:17a

For the ancient warrior, the helmet was always a crucial piece of their equipment. The nature of hand combat being what it is, a head injury was the most likely means of being incapacitated and losing one's ability to persevere in the fight. Head injuries often lead to a diminished capacity to perform as planned and this obviously could result in permanent injury or a mortal wound. At the very least, it's understood that even temporary, non-lethal head injuries that can be overcome in time, force one to retire from the task at hand. For the Roman soldier, trained, prepared and ready to perform to meet the expectations of his commander, these types of injuries are to be avoided at all cost.

Here again, the commander has provided for them. The Roman *cassius* was an evolution of technology resulting in a comprehensively effective tool of defensive capacity. Historically, the earliest helmets were made of any material available - leather and even crocodile skin was used. One of the first examples with potentially more armor-like performance, was used by the Mycenaean Greeks and made of boar's tusks. Evolving eventually into bronze designs, by the time of Paul's writing, the Roman helmet was constructed of lighter and stronger steel.

Some helmets being beautiful works of artistic design, the common soldier of the late first century used the Gallic Type 'G' or Type 'H' helmet, according to Daniel Petersen in *The Roman Legions*. The name belying its origins, these helmets bore roots in earlier examples used by the western European tribes with whom the Romans had contact by at least the early 4th century B.C..

The Romans, ever cognizant of the dangers associated with the height disparity when facing most of their enemies, sought to minimize these risks with effective equipment designs. So, as with the reinforced upper sections of the *lorica segmentata*, the helmet was fashioned to receive the impact of enemy weapons from above with little affect. It accomplished this by the use of reinforced 'eyebrow' designs above the face opening, hinged cheek plates and broad sloping rear neck guard.

Recognizing the importance of maintaining full faculties of sight and sound, the Types G and H offered a broad face aperture allowing useful wide peripheral vision. Also, ear holes were cut and protective flanges mounted above those holes to safely maintain the effective use of audible battlefield commands.

No contemporary combatant had anything as effectively protective while simultaneously being so user friendly. This is the helmet of our salvation.

Unlike the caligae of having our feet shod with the preparation of the Gospel, where our preparation (training) is emphasized, here it is salvation itself that Paul recognizes as part of the armor. Paul now is acknowledging the importance of our concession to this salvation. By naming this piece of armor as he did, the apostle identifies a critical aspect of God's relationship with His people. Namely, that the relationship is unshakeable, unbreakable and unyielding. As Andy Naselli summarizes the book *How Can I Be Sure I'm A Christian* written by Don Whitney, one's salvation is based on:

A) the character of God,
B) the works of Christ and
C) the promises of God.

The eternal security that a Christ-follower finds themselves in possession of, is based on fact. This is why

John wrote "I write these things to you who believe in the name of the Son of God so that you may know that you have eternal life." *1Jn 5:13.* John wants us to *eido - to perceive and properly see* that we *echo - hold, are possessed with and accompanied by,* the eternal life we received in Christ. Yet this truth is something to which the believer must consciously yield to because, as simple as it might be, it's quite counterintuitive to fallen humanity.

Naselli continues that, among other reasons, barriers to one's willingness to yield to confidence in salvation are:

A) spiritual immaturity
B) Sensitivity to sin

Still, we can, as JD Greear the pastor of The Summit Church in Raleigh N.C. simply instructs, "rest in the promises of God."

Ray Galea in an essay for The Gospel Coalition, instructs "Assurance springs not from the power of positive thinking but the power of the gospel." We're not saved when we feel saved or are confident in our responsive behavior before God. Galea further teaches that the opposite of belief isn't doubt but unbelief. Galea suggests doubt is present to some degree in every believer, harkening back to the rebellious nature within everyone before coming to Christ. But disbelief is different. Jesus confronted it in Mark chapter 9.

"And someone from the crowd answered him, "Teacher, I brought my son to you, for he has a spirit that makes him mute. And whenever it seizes him, it throws him down, and he foams and grinds his teeth and becomes rigid. So I asked your disciples to cast it out, and they were not able." vss *17&18*.

[And Jesus asked his father, "How long has this been happening to him?" vs *21a*.

And he said, "From childhood. And it has often cast him into fire and into water, to destroy him. But if you can do anything, have compassion on us and help us." vss *21b & 22*.

And Jesus said to him, "'**If you can!** All things are possible for one who believes." vs *23*.

Immediately the father of the child cried out and said, "I believe; help my unbelief!" vs *24*.]

If you can?! If you can?! What do you mean if you can? The father wanted to believe, but it's so foreign to the old nature without God, to even comprehend belief in God. This is what Galea meant by suggesting doubt may exist, but if one trusts God, unbelief cannot exist. Paul referred to Abraham as "being fully persuaded that God had power to do what he had promised." *Rom 4:21.* Abraham was *plerophoreo - completely assured and most assuredly believed to the point of making full proof* (by his actions) that God could fulfill His promises, regardless of Abraham's own lack of vision or understanding about how God would do it.

Trusting God

This assurance comes from trusting God for His promises and by knowing God for who He is. And who is the salvation provider? El-Shaddai – the all sufficient One, said "because, if you confess with your mouth that Jesus is

Lord and believe in your heart that God raised him from the dead, you will be saved." *Rom 10:9*. He said it will happen. It's a promise with the full power of the universe creator behind it.

Paul teaches that because of the eternal priesthood of Jesus Christ, "Consequently, he is able to save to the uttermost those who draw near to God through him, since he always lives to make intercession for them." *Heb 7:25*. Jesus being the only means to access the grace and mercy of God, the consequence of the confession and belief described in Romans 10:9 is that this same Jesus Christ, as William Magee the Irish Reformation preacher of the 1800's describes, "was not only the offering, but the priest who offered it. Therefore, He has become not only a sacrifice, but an intercessor; His intercession being founded on His voluntary offering of Himself without spot to God. We are not only then in virtue of His sacrifice forgiven, but in virtue of the intercession admitted to favor and grace." The writer of the Hebrews letter is saying that *Pantote zao - as long as Jesus is alive*, which is obviously forever, that He will be speaking to God in a legal sense to arbitrate a sentence of justification for those who confess and believe.

While the vocation by which Christ divests His privilege of negotiating the justification of His people lies in the earlier Jewish priesthood, where the ancestors of Aaron were sanctified for the purpose of seeking temporary atonement for the Jews, there were contemporary legal systems in the Roman world of Paul's time which would be more familiar to the gentile converts reading his letters. In the Roman world political power is *imperium*. This is a tiered system of power. Consuls hold more power than tribunes, who hold more power than praetors and so on. Adrian Goldsworthy explains that Emperor Augustus Caesar held *maius imperium proconsulare.* "proconsular power that was superior to all other proconsuls."

With this authority comes the privilege of *intercessio.* According to the *Dictionary of Greek and Roman Antiquities,* this allows holders of *imperium* to intercede and overrule decisions from politicians of equal or lower *imperium.* Thus Caesar Augustus could intercede on a judgment and his decision would be absolutely binding and without the possibility of that decision being revoked by anyone. So then, when the Hebrews letter writer informs that Jesus the Messiah intercedes on behalf of His followers with the result that they are 'saved to the uttermost,' even the gentiles of the Roman world have a frame of reference to understand that this intercessory judgment is *panteles - fully ended, entire and complete.* There is no higher authority that might overturn this decision. This is our salvation provider.

Once this decision is made, circumstances have changed permanently. There is no return to the old condition. To use Roman vernacular, the Rubicon has been crossed. Once judgment has been passed in heaven regarding the justification of an individual who has recognized their need for the Gospel of Christ, the individual's relationship with God has irreversibly changed. This is because of the thoughts and actions of God, not the believer, much like Julius Caesar's circumstances when he crossed the Rubicon River in northern Italy. When he did so, it was clear that he planned to march his army to Rome to assume power. Immediately after that happened, his relationship with the Roman Senate changed because of their thoughts and responses to Caesar's decision.

Just what are the responses? In Rome the senators called up Pompey the Great to gather an army representing the official Roman government to contest Caesar's intent to march his army toward Rome. In heaven there is rejoicing for every individual who is justified in Christ. Jehovah-Jireh responds by sending an additional gift; the counselor and teacher, His Holy Spirit. Paul instructs "In Him you also, when you heard the word of truth, the gospel of your salvation, and believed in him, were sealed with the promised Holy Spirit," *Eph 1:13*. Once Romans 10:9 belief is embraced, and *intercessio* is made on one's behalf by the highest priestly authority in the universe and justification judgment is passed, God chooses to *sphragizo - stamp (with a signet or private mark) for security and preservation,* the ruling. God's people are literally given the universe creator's personal seal of approval and protection. More than just a nod and a wink, this is a decisive action taken by God to send His autonomous spiritual presence to commune with every believer.

Paul further articulates God's intent by this action, "who is the guarantee of our inheritance until we acquire possession of it, to the praise of his glory." *Eph 1:14.* Amazingly, although God has already bought our justification with the sacrifice of His Son, Adonai further offers a guarantee to His commitment to adopt believers as heirs to His kingdom of heaven. The Holy Spirit is that *arrhabon - pledge given in advance as security,* until one reaches the point of possessing that inheritance.

It's because this succession of actions is driven and guaranteed by God, that Paul wrote to the Roman church, "For I am sure that neither death nor life, nor angels nor rulers, nor things present nor things to come, nor powers, nor height nor depth, nor anything else in all creation, will be able to separate us from the love of God in Christ Jesus our Lord." *Rom 8:38,39.* It's quite a comprehensive statement, including 'nor anything else in all creation,' which is built on an indefinite pronoun, that literally means any physical thing you can possibly imagine. For one to be separated specifically from the salvation–of–Christ–based love of God, would require as Roman law would indicate, a magisterial authority higher than the One who justifies God's people. That authority just doesn't exist.

Further, God's seal of guarantee is no trifle. He didn't offer a trinket ring or embossed clay cylinder that might be discarded if one grows weary of their relationship with God. Since no one can dictate the activities of the Holy Spirit, not even the beneficiary of God's grace can reverse the impact of being reborn in Christ. Not by words, or actions, or force of will, or temper tantrums or even by subsequent commitments to oppose God. The love of

God and His promises are too complete and perfect to be undermined by the emotional inconsistency of any part of God's creation. The Holy Spirit will remain until possession of God's promised inheritance is realized. Therefore, one's direct relationship with Immanuel will remain. This too is our salvation provider.

We can recognize the difference here between this confidence we have in the salvation Christ provides, and faith that compels one to action with the expectation of God's ordained outcome. Faith in what God will do versus knowledge of what He has done.

As we've seen through understanding the use of the Roman *scutum*, faith is an action based derivative of our confidence in God. Its purpose is to create a foundation by which one can conquer new territory for God's kingdom. From the beginning, even salvation faith from God is the means by which the action of belief in God unto salvation is driven, the new territory of one's soul is taken from the enemies of God and becomes part of His kingdom. After that, faith continues to be the evidence of things not seen and the reason for a willingness to participate in further new experiences on the path of following God.

Once the new experience is completed, like one's justification in Christ, it becomes fact. Does it need further faith to trust it? The completed matter becomes part of one's base of knowledge and experience, like the Roman soldier's previous battles, to provide useful insight into future events. This knowledge no longer requires faith to understand since the insight has been gained by empirical evidence. We should consider our salvation in Christ this way, and can relate most subsequent experiences thus also.

Therefore our salvation is based on faith in God's promises, and then known as fact based on the evidence of our experiences with God through the Holy Spirit.

Nonetheless, Ray Galea warns, the goal of all God's enemies is to create unbelief in Christ followers and "hijack their confidence." Because of this Galea continues, the "Christian's pursuit of assurance is a matter of spiritual warfare." The mind of the believer is territory that any one of the enemies of God must conquer to meet Clausewitz's required goals of being victorious in warfare; destroying the enemy's power and taking possession of the enemy's assets.

Paul is teaching the Ephesian church that knowing with full certainty, the secure reality of our salvation in Christ, is protection against the work of God's enemies. In the prosecution of one's service in God's kingdom and their priesthood, believers can focus on faith-based obedience to God leading their daily activities and spiritual warfare, because they don't have to continually revisit past struggles.

Soldiers that struggle with memories of previous battles are diagnosed to have PTSD (post-traumatic stress disorder). This condition makes it difficult or sometimes impossible to function effectively in any further plans their commander might have. This is exactly the result of doubt in the salvation power of Christ and the promises of God to guarantee it. When one must continually fight the enemy on the ground of the believer's heart and mind, which is territory that Christ already won, then God's enemies benefit by delaying any possibility of that believer having any impact on the proliferation of God's influence.

Instead we can better know God through His gracious commitment, recognize Christ as the catalyst and completer of salvation, and experience the Holy Spirit as the immovable anchor point of a new life in Christ.

The thorough protection offered by the *Cassius* Type H helmet is a befitting illustration for the safeguard in spiritual warfare that God offers believers through the absolute surety one may possess of the salvation received through Jesus Christ. More a passive defense, when the helmet is worn properly, it's not something to be handled in battle as it does its job so the user can focus on the work of taking ground from the enemy. For the believer, salvation is worked out so when the Christ-follower is adorned by it, there is no need to tamper with it. One can focus on the path, work, priesthood and spiritual warfare of seeking first the kingdom of God with confidence in the commander.

"Let us then with confidence draw near to the throne of grace, that we may receive mercy and find grace to help in time of need." *Heb 4:16.*

CHAPTER 9

THE SWORD OF THE SPIRIT

"and the sword of the Spirit, which is the
word of God"

Eph 6:17b

Finally we come to the primary offensive tool of the Roman legionnaire. Though there are other weapons available and used in every battle, the sword *gladius*, is the fundamental element to the success of the soldier. The javelin *pilum,* and dagger *pugio*, were often useful but always secondary to the execution of their efforts. Even the shield, used offensively, would upset the enemy by knocking them off balance and possibly sending them reeling backward and allowing the Roman to step forward to take and occupy another step of territory from the enemy. But ultimately it was only the sword which could decisively dispatch the enemy and remove the threat against the empire.

The *gladius* has its roots in the Celt-Iberian culture of early Spain. Rome being a melting pot of culture much like the United States, often foreign designs were adopted and modified to suit Roman requirements. In this case, the results were one of the most feared and respected weapons of the ancient world.

Though there were a few variants, the *gladius* generally consisted of a blade about 24 inches, with the grip and hilt roughly an additional 6 inches. The hilt always terminated in a pronounced pommel that performed as a counterweight to the blade. While some *gladii* blades were straight edged and others were wasp waisted, all bore sharp edges on both sides in conjunction with the sharply pointed tip.

Due to the nature of Roman combat, the *gladius* required unique and precise specifications. It was a thrusting weapon in the hands of the legionnaire as the ancient historian Vegetius describes, "They were likewise taught not to cut but to thrust with their swords. For the Romans not only made a jest of those who fought with the edge of that weapon, but always found them an easy conquest." However given the nature of hand combat it would surely, according to Adrian Goldsworthy in *Roman Warfare*, be used to slash and cut on occasion and so must be built to function in that manner also. It must be well balanced so that during prolonged engagements, continued thrusting motion would not fatigue the soldier and lead to the unintentional lowering of the blade tip thus missing the target.

Back then there were no measuring calipers, temperature gauges or gas fired forges. Even still, the *gladii* blades were sized perfectly. The hilts were perfectly weighted. The full tang, blade spine and edges were differentially tempered to perfection, to guarantee the sword wouldn't bend, brake or chip during strenuous use.

It was a consummately reliable tool. That these craftsmen could create tools of such high excellence is still a marvel to modern blacksmiths.

As we have seen, there was no enemy against whom the *gladius* was not the right tool.

This is the Word of God to which Paul refers using climactic visual imagery. For all the power of Rome, the hundreds of thousands of legionnaires, and the inexhaustible wealth powering their economy, it was ultimately the *gladius* which purveyed that power. For the Christ follower, it is the Word of God which imparts God's power in spiritual warfare.

Where does the Word of God fit into the life of the believer? When the soldier received his shoes and belt, he knew his life would be different, and when he received his shield he knew he'd be a conqueror. When he was given his helmet and breastplate he knew he would be protected. But when he was given the sword he knew he'd destroy his commander's enemies.

On our own we might not conceive the Word of God this way but this is the imagery that Paul uses. It's God's message found throughout the New Testament. The benefit is not the destructive capability of the Word, but the valuable results upon utilizing it. Yet do believers hold even the same regard for the word as the Roman soldier did for his *gladius*?

A Living and Powerful Word

We now have the benefit of this New Covenant perspective of the Word. No longer is it a lexicon of laws accompanied by histories and prophecies whose end goal is to control behavior. Sometime during the reign of Augustus Caesar and Herod, a child was born as described by those prophecies. It soon became apparent that this child was God. John explains, "In the beginning was the Word, and the Word was with God, and the Word was God .... And the Word became flesh and dwelt among us, and we have seen his glory, glory as of the only Son from the Father, full of grace and truth." *Jn 1:1-14.* Matthew Henry describes this as "The Word had a being before the world had a beginning. He that was in the beginning never began, and therefore was ever, *achronos—without beginning of time.* Looking at the specific nature of the Greek 'word' *logos,* it suggests not merely thought, information or knowledge, but the actionable expressions of God: *to speak, to reason, to compute, cause communication, etc.* In the context of John's discourse, *logos* is the Divine Expression (of action). Thus, He spoke the world into existence.

Then the Word 'became flesh' and dwelt among humanity and Jesus became the physical manifestation of that expose´. He is a corporeal form of Divine Expression. Now we can see that the words aren't just a table of laws and stories and proverbs, but an exposition of God with whom we can relate and have fellowship. The writings that followed, then completed the literary revelation of the essence of the triune YaHWeH. The Word of God was created by the most masterful craftsman in the universe, because it represents the expression of the perfect creator. This is actually the Word Paul is referring to. How does that fit into the life of the believer?

The Apostle Paul is instructing the reality that this written expose´ is full of knowledge and principle that can carry one through a successful pursuit of God on the path of His plans. In the context of spiritual warfare the Word purveys the power of God to thoroughly address any struggle at hand. If the *logos* is powerful enough to create the universe then it's reasonable to expect it can oversee God's people through spiritual warfare.

There is no enemy or circumstance against whom the Word of God is not the right tool. In the words of the wise woman to whom I'm married, the one relevant question to ask when faced with a difficult situation is: "What does the Word say?"

Paul rejoiced with believers when he observed a healthy relationship between them and God's Word. "And we also thank God constantly for this, that when you received the word of God, which you heard from us, you accepted it not as the word of men but as what it really is, the word of God, which is at work in you believers." *1 Thess 2:13*. Here Paul is identifying the desired end state of God's Word with the Christian. That being, it becomes *energeo - active, fervently effectual, mighty in showing forth itself in working* in the believer, most likely in the ways Paul explains the Word is 'profitable.'

God wants us to learn how to utilize His Word. Paul instructs Timothy, "All Scripture is breathed out by God and profitable for teaching, for reproof, for correction, and for training in righteousness," *2 Tim 3:16*. As a reminder, the preserved word of scripture was, regardless of the human authors that made the motions of penmanship, created by God as if each word was physically exhaled from Him. Just for this reality alone the Word is profitable for the stated reasons. Thus when the scripture is used properly it can be recognized that the Lord is doing the teaching, reproving, correcting and training.

It achieves these ends by virtue of that power beheld in the Word of God. Even today, the power of God is manifest through the personal revelation of scripture as Fred Zaspel describes in a book review for The Gospel Coalition (TGC), "as God spoke to Abraham and to Noah, so he speaks to us today via his written Word."

Looking at how Paul says scripture is profitable, he clearly means for the *logos - Divine Expression* to be an important foundational structure in the life of the believer. Something that consumes a large footprint of time and space in the existence of the Christ follower. As Beth sings "I have stored up your word in my heart, that I might not sin against you. Blessed are you, O Lord teach me your statutes! With my lips I declare all the rules of your mouth. In the way of your testimonies I delight as much as in all riches. I will meditate on your precepts and fix my eyes on your ways. I will delight in your statutes; I will not forget your word." *Ps 119:11-16*. Here we can see several of Paul's suggested benefits of God's Word and how they can be manifest in one's life. It's useful for the Word to be occupying space in the believer's mind. It imparts God's wisdom which is worth seeking. It's beneficial to take time repeating to others. It is as satisfying as any and all worldly riches. It's worth taking time to meditate upon. It brings joy and is worth memorizing.

Later in that song, Mem and Nun sing about their

various valuation and benefits from God's Word. Mem also loves it and meditates on it. It gives knowledge and with it, the wisdom to employ it. Mem is committed to engaging with the instruction he received. After receiving instruction from God, one comes to recognize what right looks like in the opinion of Jehovah-Tsidkenu the Righteous One, and upon realizing the benefit of following Him, it's natural to develop contempt for any deviation from His way and even the temptation of it. Thinking back to Paul's words in Romans chapter seven, this contempt doesn't always translate to perfectly righteous behavior of God's people, but valuing God enough to hate the false 'way' is a good place to start, from which to follow God. Ps 119:*97-104*.

Nun follows up by recognizing that on that path of seeking God, "Your word is a lamp to my feet and a light to my path." vs *105*. It's this path on which we previously discussed that God is establishing, that God's *logos* will illuminate a spotlight on the steps of His perfect will and even provide a floodlight to show us as much of the path as He has prepared us for. But how can we be sure about what we see illuminated or even God's will for us? Building principle upon principle, let's revisit Paul's instruction of *Rom 12:1&2*. God has told us that if we are willing to give Him what He wants: which is nothing less than ourselves, then we can *dokimazo - test to approve, discern, prove/try* what is God's plan. By seeking God as He desires for us, we can realize by empirical evidence what His path looks like for us.

Jesus pragmatically emphasized the practical benefit of engaging with God's Word. But he said, "Blessed rather are those who hear the word of God and keep it!" *Lk 11*:28. Given the way Jesus made this statement, it's not something that the believer even needs to hope for. It's fact. It's a commitment by God that He has executed already. If a condition of 'hear & keep' exists, then the Word of God is 'fervently effectual,' so a state of *makarios - supremely blessed, well-off* can exist in the believer. This too can be a point of contact in spiritual warfare. None of the enemies of God want to see a *makarios* condition in anyone's life. We can remember that they (satan, self or others) desire to be the focal point of power and worship. Though they can't steal the blessing, they will attempt to steal the peace of this *makarios* from the Christ follower.

Keeping in mind the context of Paul's Ephesian message, we can concurrently be aware that the believer's relationship with the Word of God, is meant to be embraced and 'active' within the community setting of the believer's life. We've discussed how God intends for the Christian's path of seeking Him is to be traveled within the framework of church unity.

And so mechanisms of Jehovah-Jireh provide for His Word, a means to operate in harmony with the body of Christ. Paul shares a glimpse of what this looks like in his letter to Colosse. "Let the word of Christ dwell in you richly, teaching and admonishing one another in all wisdom, singing psalms and hymns and spiritual songs, with thankfulness in your hearts to God." *Col 3:16*. When the Word of God occupies adequate headspace and personal time, Paul refers to this condition as 'dwelling in you richly.' Given all we've previously discussed, we can now look at this phrase in the original language to realize a greater impact of its message. *Logos Christos enoikeo en humin plausios*. The Divine expression that has existed eternally who took on corporeal form in Jesus the Christ *logos Christos*, who now resides in heaven with the Father, will inhabit and occupy space with one of His created human beings *enoikeo en humin*, copiously in abundantly rich manner *plousios*.

Matthew Henry describes the impact of this 'dwelling' of the Word. "It is ready at hand to have its due and influence in us." And, Henry continues, will "enable us to conduct ourselves in everything as becomes children of wisdom."

The writer of the Hebrew letter in chapter 4 instructs that the root cause of someone being disqualified from entering eternal rest with God is the obedience to the nature into which we are born. It follows then, he teaches, those who enter God's rest will be God's people who were obedient instead, to the good news of the Gospel. How is the evaluation conducted between children of disobedience and Matthew Henry's children of wisdom?

"For the word of God is living and active, sharper than any two-edged sword, piercing to the division of soul and of spirit, of joints and of marrow, and discerning the thoughts and intentions of the heart. And no creature is hidden from his sight, but all are naked and exposed to the eyes of him to whom we must give account." *Heb 4:12-13.*

It's actually possible to comprehend how Elohim the all-powerful creator appraises judgment: all things are weighed by the word of God. The same word that He has preserved for His creation to profit from. The same word that can dwell in us richly.

While these verses might seem ominous to God's creation, unable to hide from the judge, and exposed as naked to the judge's eyes. Well that we should reckon these words fearsome, but for those who are reborn in obedience to the call of the Gospel, the Hebrews writer declares, they will enter the eternal rest with God. Case closed.

Further, we can see in verse twelve how the word of God performs its function in the appraisal of good and bad, right and wrong, obedient and disobedient.

1. it is alive, *zao - living, possessing life*. As it has since before the beginning of our timeline. As it had when taking on flesh and dwelling among humanity and resuming residence in heaven. As it does when it chooses to reside in God's people.

2. It's busy – *energes* - *active and operative with power.* As it imparts knowledge and wisdom to God's people. As it guides the corporate functions of the church and every single footstep of every single person seeking Him.

3. It utilizes its power with pinpoint accuracy to supreme affect – *tomoteros* - *to cut, but more comprehensively and decisively, by implication, with a single stroke.* It's more keen. It sees more, knows more and beholds more power. More than any other source of knowledge, appraisal and influence in the history of creation. More effective than even the revered *gladius.*

Eric Raymond of Emmaus Bible Church, writing for TGC, ponders, "You would expect a book that is divine and living would in fact be active, and so it is." It's fervently effective in a copious manner.

We're beginning to see here that with all the profitable qualities and function of the Word of God, *logos* - *The Divine Expression* has been weaponized for God's people. It's a multi-purpose tool, but it's a weapon of the highest caliber for those engaged in spiritual warfare.

Not merely cutting the bone and soft tissue, as Matthew Henry describes, it "enters where no other sword can, and makes a more critical dissection," the division of soul and spirit. It is, after all, the tool by which is illuminated the judgment of condemnation or justification. But that's how it performs when utilized by El Roi – God who sees all.

When it's employed by those in whom the Word dwells

richly, it discerns the thoughts and intents of the heart. It is therefore possible for the Christian to gain wisdom and insight to the thoughts, motives and intentions hidden in oneself and even in others. Particularly the enemies with whom one might be contending with in spiritual warfare. What a valuable asset this becomes when engaged in spiritual conflict.

In fact King Solomon identified this maxim thousands of years ago, "But I say that wisdom is better than might" *Ecc 9:18a*. The wise king recognized that any physical strength or the power given by the use of well crafted weapons, is no match against great wisdom applied to the tools one might have at hand. As Solomon had mentioned previously in that same chapter, that battle is not given to the strong people who fight. He recognizes that anyone can be 'snared' during an evil day. But he continues that it requires wisdom, not physical abilities to overcome those evil days. Sounds exactly like what Paul is teaching.

There has been a resurgence in modern military theory to recognize the importance of the independent performance capability of small combat units. This is something that the Roman legions emphasized as did many of the best performing military organizations throughout history. Recent theorists have attempted to define, and quantify this important dynamic of successful warfare.

Battle Wisdom and Spiritual Warfare

Dr. Irv Lachow, Mr. David Gompert, Mr. Justin Perkins (LGP) wrote a report for the National Defense University at Fort Lesley J. McNair, called *Battle-Wisdom. Improving Cognitive Performance in Network Centric Warfare.* In it they recognize the fact that there might be many combat operations and certainly numerous logistical activities being carried out concurrently at any given time. This is true on a broad strategic level or even a more localized tactical level. Thus the better a military organization can coordinate these operations, the more likely to achieve success. This they call, a network centric warfare.

It also describes the actual state of existence of all those seeking God. What every believer does and experiences every day is part of a broad network of activity that encompasses Jehovah's plan. Likewise this is true with an impact on strategic and local implications. As we have seen, it is God's plan for His people to work with and within this spiritual network centric activity as He leads the organizational body – the church.

Because of this complexity of activity, impact is felt by even the smallest denomination of unit, thereby emphasizing the importance of performance by even the lowest ranking personnel.

LGP explain the impact of this. "Decisions that were once made by colonels are being made by captains and the consequences of those decisions are having global impacts. It is imperative that the U.S. military improve the ability of soldiers to make quick, accurate, and reliable decisions in complex, dynamic and ambiguous situations. To do so, soldiers must be able to move between formal reasoning and intuitive decision making quickly and seamlessly. We call this ability "battle-wisdom" and believe that it may be a decisive factor in determining the outcome of future conflicts." The authors of the report say nothing of the weapons in use, but suggest instead that the cognitive functions of the combatant will control the conflict and bring success by effectively making all the correct decisions about time, place, employment of available tools and use of knowledge (training).

The authors also advocate that it's the leadership's responsibility to impart this wisdom to all combatants, and those who represent the effective power and threat to the enemy. "Increased access to information, if it is gathered, processed, analyzed, filtered and presented properly, can certainly improve decision-making."

Christians should recognize that the spiritual warfare combat leadership of the church, Jehovah-Jireh, God-will-provide, has since the day of that first pentecost after Jesus ascended to heaven, done exactly what the report authors (LGP) have identified as the means to obtain victory in warfare. Particularly nowadays, we have better access than ever before to the needed information since the written Word is now so prolific. Those seeking God can gather the information. It can be sought through committing time to read the Word, and also through the help of the body of Christ with whom one is working. The question is are Christians even trying. The information can then be "processed, analyzed, filtered and presented properly" through the guidance of the Divine Counselor, the Holy Spirit. That, the authors inform, will 'certainly' lead to improved cognitive functions during conflict. Thus using LGB's theory, we can see how the wisdom of God gives Christians 'battle wisdom'.

As we're often told, our battle is not against flesh and

blood, but of spiritual nature, wisdom from God is even more impactful than the brute force of a soldier on the battlefield. Paul actually disparages the value of the *gladius* in the employ of the Roman soldier, (sharper than any two-edged sword) compared to the value of the wisdom of God in spiritual warfare. It would be helpful then for those engaged in spiritual conflict to remember that it's important not to dwell on the physical nature of what is seen, and instead focus on the spiritual impact of God's *energeo*.

Perhaps this is what Paul was thinking when he wrote to the Corinthian believers, "For the weapons of our warfare are not of the flesh but have divine power to destroy strongholds." *2 Cor 10:4*. Even though our weapons are not of the flesh, they still destroy strongholds. How is this possible?

Again thinking back to Joshua's experience at Jericho, God gave him the knowledge of His battle plan, and Joshua employed the wisdom God had given him, from the knowledge and experiences he gained by following God since they left Egypt 40+ years before. This wisdom informed Joshua that he should obey these wild and far-fetched instructions from his Captain.

The most important question from that event might be: if the Israelites hadn't marched around the city the way the Captain ordered, would the walls have fallen? To summarize the entire Bible to answer that; no. The walls would not have fallen. We can then, like Paul, downplay the value of the physical walls falling around Jericho (details for which there is significant archaeological evidence) and recognize the importance of the increased cognitive ability gained by the wisdom of God, that led to the decision to obey the Captain. By this, spiritual weapons affected the physical world.

These things still happen today, as Paul continued to explain to the Corinthians, "We destroy arguments and every lofty opinion raised against the knowledge of God, and take every thought captive to obey Christ" *vs 5*. The spiritual weapons available to us from God, and specifically because of its impact on our 'battle-wisdom," the sword of the spirit which is the Word of God will literally and figuratively impact the physical world. It will do so by effectively interdicting the work of all the enemies, and Paul is rather specific as to how.

The wisdom found in God's Word will *kathaireo - demolish, cast down and destroy* all of the enemy's *logismos - computation, reasoning and imaginative thought*. It will expose all of the secretive, deceptive and calculated manipulations of the fallen host as they attempt to undermine the influence of YaHWeH in the world. Like any battle plan, once it's known, it can be outwitted and prevented. Similarly the wisdom of God's Word will frustrate the sentiments and judgments issued from a world full of individuals that are rebellious against God, which is assumed to be more valuable than God. The folly of these sentiments and judgments can be exposed thereby informing the Christ follower toward conduct in keeping with the knowledge of God.

Further it can effectively control the battle against the final enemy. That dangerous and shocking enemy with seemingly independent freedom of thought; our old nature void of God and seeking to satiate itself. The wisdom of

God's Word can 'seize by force or skill' every thought within oneself. Perhaps the most profound application of 'battle-wisdom' is the ability we find in Christ to perform, that which Paul said he himself couldn't even do: to take command of action and thought from our own fallen nature.

Jamieson, Fausset and Brown (JFB) in their *Commentary Critical and Explanitory on the Whole Bible*, point out that this is something different than how we find the end result of the effect of God's wisdom applied to the other spiritual enemies. With the others, the work of their warfare is met with destruction and resigned to the oblivion of uselessness. However with this enemy of self, it's not God's intent to 'cast down' their effective value. Instead according to JFB, God desires, through the wisdom of His Word, to "tender the voluntary obedience of faith to Christ the Conqueror."

Eric Raymond says of it, "Because it is God's word, it is an undefeatable word. The Bible has all the essentials of the life and power of God to do his work!" We can take that literally. There is no weapon available to any of the enemies of God that can overcome the sword of the Spirit which is the Word of God. As the principal offensive weapon in the panoply of equipment that God has given His people, it's essential to recognize the value and usage for which God has intended His Word in the life of those seeking God.

"But thanks be to God, who in Christ always leads us in triumphal procession, and through us spreads the fragrance of the knowledge of him everywhere."

2 Cor 2:14.

It's 70 A.D.. The ancient historian Josephus is in Rome to witness the greatest spectacle of his life. It starts outside the gates of the city.

"During the hours of darkness the whole military

225

force had been led out in companies and battalions by its officers… For Titus and Vespasian had spent the night there, and now, as dawn began to break, they emerged, crowned in laurel wreaths and wearing the time-honored purple clothes…

As they walked forward to take their seats, all the soldiers raised an immediate cheer, paying abundant testimony to their valor, while Titus and Vespasian sat unarmed, dressed in silk garments and wearing their laurel wreaths. Vespasian acknowledged their acclaim… Afterward, donning the triumphal robes and sacrificing to the gods stationed at the gate, they sent the procession on its way through the theaters to give the crowds a better view.

It is impossible to do justice in the description of the number of things to be seen and to the magnificence of everything that met the eye, whether in skilled craftsmanship, staggering richness or natural rarity. …but resembled, as it were, a running river of wealth.

The greatest amazement was caused by the floats. Their size gave grounds for alarm about their stability, for many were three or four stories high, and in the richness of their manufacture they provided an astonishing and pleasurable sight.

The procession was completed by Vespasian, and, behind him, Titus." Josephus, *Wars of the Jews Book 7.*

The Roman 'triumph' was a great event in the ancient Mediterranean world. It was an experience granted by the government to a military commander who victoriously concluded a war on behalf of Rome. In an article of the Villanova University library online, it's suggested that "the triumph was the honor that men dreamt of achieving. It was thought to be the pinnacle of the Roman military, and often political, career. The general himself was supposed to be the main attraction..." And as Mary Beard writes in *The Roman Triumph,* "the triumph, in other words, re-presented and re-enacted victory. It brought the margins of the empire to its center."

The commander, as Vespasian and his son Titus who also led the war, rode in an elevated chariot and were so garbed as to very specifically represent the Roman deity Jupiter Optimus Maximus - Jupiter best and greatest. So literal was this imagery taken, that an additional passenger stood behind them whose job was to whisper in their ear that they're yet mortal humans.

Spoils of the campaign led the parade procession. In the case of Pompey the Great's triumph parade, there were so many spoils, that the parade took two days to complete. In Vespasian's triumph, the spoils came from Jerusalem and its temple, and were so valuable as to fully provide the funding to build the great colosseum in Rome that stands today.

Following the commander and his procession, came his soldiers who participated in the campaign. As they marched through the streets of Rome, they sang songs about their leader whose day of veneration this was. The soldiers were blissful. They were grown wealthy from the grace of their commander who shared the spoils of war with them. The fighting men were also proud of their accomplishments, to have vanquished those the commander identified as an enemy. Proud to have endured the hardship, and shared camaraderie with their commander. They knew they wouldn't be there without him.

Reading Josephus' description with all the lofty grandeur, one might mistake it for a passage from John's Revelation as a picture of heaven. We can indeed recognize the self aggrandizement of all the deific overtones and display of wealth as yet another attempt to replace God with the worship of self.

Again Paul is using here, historical information commonplace in the life of the Roman Empire. He captures imagery of ordinary knowledge to ripen wisdom from God in the mind of contemporary believers. This imagery is worth revisiting for the modern Christian to grasp the precision and depth of Paul's message.

In the modern vernacular of the American gospel, one would be tempted to assume the focus of the triumphal parade that Paul describes would be the Christ-follower. As if it was our triumph.

In fact Paul said that Christ will lead us in *thriambeuo - an acclamatory procession of victory*. Christ leads us in the procession where we honor, applaud and celebrate, not ourselves in the likeness of Vespasian, but His victory as the *vir triumphalis - man of triumph*. Recognizing that the imagery that Paul uses is of the Roman triumph, it's easier to properly see that the believer's place in the procession is behind the leader, and singing songs about him. The event is about the victorious leader: Christ the Captain of the army of God, as Joshua knew Him, our commander in spiritual warfare. He is The *vir triumphalis*. One that makes no apology for His deity. Like the Roman soldiers, we can be thankful and blessed to participate in His triumph since we too are benefactors of the commander's grace and generosity.

For the born again, Christ following, seeker of the path of God, this is the only possible outcome of the trouble, conflict and spiritual warfare they might experience. This is because, for all the reasons we've discussed thus far, there is no power in creation that can undermine the will of God or His promises to His people, despite the frailties of humanity and the current allowances given for sin to run its course. Dudley Hall of Kerygma Ventures instructs "We fight with weapons that cannot be matched by the forces of evil or the schemes of the world."

God has made provision for the proper equipment of His people. It's already done and given. There is no need to find a Christian quartermaster to whom one must give justification in asking for the armor of God. Christ has given it already. It's His armor. It comes from His life, work and inherent nature. Though the believer might initially consider it easier to wear other armor, one might follow David's example. Had he worn the armor Saul offered him instead of using what God had provided (the sling and his skill to use it), the outcome would have assuredly been much different.

It requires specific thought to don the armor of God, but when one does so, they are putting on Jesus Christ. To put on *enduo - array oneself with clothing* for protection and display, the life, work and nature of Christ. The ability to do so is actually a privilege every believer can take for granted because it's based on God's commitment to us.

Jehovah-Jireh has also offered the means to access knowledge and wisdom to properly utilize the tools and armor of God. The Holy Counselor and Comforter, sent by God for the benefit of His people. Not so much a response to our decisions, God chooses to send the Holy Spirit based on His promises.

Thus equipped, Christ followers can train to operate as God has planned for His people. They can choose to ignore the need to train, or train casually, or follow the example of the Roman illustration with its clear results, and train rigorously in Christ.

And the church might well be conscientious of the value of experience. Capitalize on it by maintaining it in our memory. Nurture it by the use of memorials as was done in the Old Testament.

"As the church, in response to various culture wars, increasingly turns to numerous battles 'with flesh and blood' rather than to the primary battle with 'the spiritual forces of wickedness in the heavenly places' *Eph. 6:12*, one must wonder if we have forgotten the teaching of the New Testament itself." John H. Armstrong *The Coming Evangelical Crisis*. Yet as training and experience develop in the believer, they become more adept at recognizing the true nature of trouble and conflict in their lives. So then the empowerment of God can steel one to successfully engage in the conflict.

Is there anywhere else one might turn to meet with success in the ways that matter in life? As Peter said to Jesus, "Lord, to whom shall we go? You have the words of eternal life. We have come to believe and to know that you are the Holy One of God." *Jn 6:68-69*. This is a brief yet succinct way of articulating that when life is refined down the few objects of importance, the Lord Jesus Christ is the single and unique source of meeting the needs of those objects.

> "Lord, may your people grow to act like they've come to believe and know that You are the Holy One of God." Amen.

"But blessed is the one who trusts in the LORD, whose confidence is in him."

Jer 17:7

GLOSSARY OF HISTORICAL FIGURES AND NON-ENGLISH WORDS

Alexander the Great – (356 BC – 323 BC) born Alexander III of Macedon. Tutored by Aristotle. Forged and empire spanning from Greece to India. Died aged 32.

Anothen – Greek, Strong's ref. 509, from above again.

Appian of Alexandria – (95 AD – 165 AD) Greek historian who received Roman citizenship. Held political offices and practices law as a legal advocate.

Apoluo – Greek, Strong's ref. 630, released, set free, at liberty.

Araw – Hebrew, Strong's ref. 781. Espouse, engage for matrimony.

Arche - Greek, Strong's ref. 746, magistrate power, rule.

Archegos – Greek, Strong's ref. 747, chief leader, Captain.

Arrhabon – Greek, Strong's ref. 728. A pledge that is part of a purchase given in advance as security for the rest.

Arminius – (18 BC – 21 AD) Chieftain the the Germanic Cherusci tribe. Serve3d in the Roman army as an ally with Roman citizenship. Secretly defected to lead an ambush that destroyed three Roman legions.

Augustus Caesar – (69 BC – 14 AD) known as Gaius Julius Caesar Augustus. Born Gaius Octavius. Adopted by Julius Caesar. First proper Roman Emperor. His reign was known as the *Pax Romana*, the time of Roman peace.

Aqob – Hebrew, Strong's ref. 6121, fraudulent, deceitful, polluted.

Balteus – Latin, Belt.

Caligae - *plural for caliga - Latin,* shoes. Specifically the military style, hobnailed, boot–like open toe sandal used by Roman soldiers of the 1st century AD.

Cambyses – (6th century BC) Cambyses II. Achaemenid Dynasty, ruled the Persian Empire 550 BC – 530 BC. Son of Cyrus the Great.

Carl Von Clausewitz – (1780 – 1831) born Carl Philipp Gottlieb Von Clausewitz. A Prussian general best known as a theorist. His treatise, *Vom Kriege,* On War, is mandatory reading for anyone studying the art of war.

Cassius – Latin, helmet.

Centurio – Latin, roughly equivalent to modern Captain.

Charis – Greek, Strong's ref. 5485, grace, Divine influence upon the heart.

Chashab – Hebrew, Strong's ref. 2803, to weave or fabricate, to plot or contrive.

Cippi – Latin, a low, stone pedestal set up as a mile marker or boundary marker.

Cleopatra (70 BC – 30 BC) known as Cleopatra VII Thea Philopater. Descendant of one of Alexander the Great's generals. Last Ptolemaic Egyptian ruler. Politically and personally influential in the life and career of Julius Caesar and Marc Antony.

Commilitones – Latin, fellow soldiers.

Contuburnium – Latin, literal translation 'tenting together'. Refers to an eight man squad of soldiers.

Dokimazo – Greek, Strong's ref. 1381. To test, allow, discern, examine, try, prove.

Dunamis – Greek, Strong's ref. 1411, miraculous power.

Echo – Greek, Strong's ref. 2192. Hold, are possessed with, accompanied by.

Eido – Greek, Strong's ref. 1492. Perceive and properly see.

El-Elyon - Hebrew, descriptive name for YHWH. The Most High God.

El-Roi - The Lord who sees all.

El-Shaddai - Hebrew with Akkadian, Canaanite roots. Descriptive name of YHWH, God Almighty, The all sufficient One, God of the Mountain.

Elohim - Hebrew, descriptive name of YHWH. The All-Powerful One, Creator.

Endunamoo en kurios - Greek, Strong's ref. 1743, 1722, 2962. Be strong in the Lord.

Enduo - Greek, Strong's ref. 1746. To array oneself with clothing, as if for protection and display.

Enduo panoplia theos - Greek, Strong's ref. 1746, 3833, 2316. Put on the whole armor of God.

Energeo - Greek, Strong's ref. 1754. Be active, be mighty, show forth self work.

Energes - Greek, Strong's ref. 1756. Active and operative with power.

Epi pas - Greek, Strong's ref. 1909, 3956. Above all, figuratively, in all things.

Frederick the Great - (1712 - 1786) Prussian Monarch Frederick II. Accomplished military commander and author.

Gaius Marius – (157 BC – 86 BC) Roman statesman and military commander. Elected Consul seven times, known for his military leadership skills.

Gladius, gladii (pl) – Latin, short double edged sword of the type used by Roman soldiers.

Hagios – Greek, Strong's ref. 40, sacred, physically pure, morally blameless, holy.

Hannibal – (247 BC – 181 BC) born Hannibal Barca. Carthaginian military commander during the 2nd Punic War. Attacked Italy leading elephants over the Alpine mountain range. Defeated several Roman armies. Returned to North Africa to be defeated by Scipio Africanus.

Haustafel – German, literally – house table. Used to refer to the table of rules to be performed by each member of a household. Used by Martin Luther to describe the various lists of rules laid out in scripture.

Hetiomazo – Greek, Strong's ref. 2090. Prepare, provide to make ready.

Herodotus – (484 BC – 425 BC) Greek historian and geographer from the city of Halicarnassus in modern Turkey. Famous for his book *Histories*.

Intercessio – Latin, legal term used to describe a governing authority to intercede on behalf of a defendant.

Jehovah – A vocalization of the name of God YHWH. A 16th century German translator wrote the name of God using the vowels of Adonai because the ancient text he was using had the vowels written below the consonants of YHWH. (YaHoVaH).

Jehovah-Jireh – Hebrew, descriptive name of YHWH. The Lord will Provide.

Jehovah-Nissi – Hebrew, descriptive name of YHWH, The Lord is my Banner.

Jehovah-Sabaoth – Hebrew, descriptive name of YHWH. Lord of armies, Lord of Hosts.

Jehovah-Shammah – Hebrew, descriptive name of YHWH. God our companion.

Jehovah-Tsidkenu – Hebrew, descriptive name of YHWH, God the righteous.

Josephus (37 AD – 100 AD) Born Flavius Josephus. Jewish military commander and historian. Surrendered in battle to soon-to-be-emperor Vespasian. Became a slave and then freed thereby taking the name Flavius. Advisor to Vespasian's son Titus.

Julius Caesar – (100 BC – 44 BC) born Gaius Julius Caesar. Roman statesman and military commander renowned for his generalship. Attained perpetual dictatorship.

Katergazomai hapas - Greek, Strong's ref. 2716, 537. Cause to do, perform work fully to accomplish, absolutely all and everything possible.

Kathaireo - Greek, Strong's ref. 2507. Demolish, tear down, destroy.

Kleronomos - Greek, Strong's ref. 2818, heir, inheritor.

Kosmokrator - Greek, Strong's ref. 2888, epithet of Satan.

Kun - Hebrew, Stong's ref. 3559, set up, appoint, render prosperous, prepare, make ready.

Lucius Aemilius Paullus Macedonicus - (229 BC - 160 BC) Roman statesman and military leader. Captured the Macedonian king Perseus in battle. Friend of the historian Polybius. Not to be confused with his father who was killed in the battle of Cannae.

Labienus - (100 BC - 45 BC) born Titus Labienus. Roman statesman and military commander. Served under the command of Julius Caesar until giving support to the Roman Senate and serving under Pompey.

Legatus Legionis - Latin, legionary commander, political appointee, requires previously held rank of Tribune.

Logismos - Greek, Strong's ref. 3053. Computation, reasoning and imaginative thought.

Logos – Greek, Strong's ref. 3056. Something said, reasoned, computed. Specifically used about God, the Divine Expression.

Logos Christos enoikeo en humin plausios – Greek, Strong's ref. 3056, 5547, 1744, 1722, 5213, 4146. The word of Christ dwell in you richly.

Lorica Segmentata – Latin, literally segmented armor. Term used to refer to to common body armor of 1st century AD Roman soldiers. It is unknown what the original users called it.

Machseh – Hebrew, Strong's ref. 4268, place of shelter, hope refuge.

Maius imperium proconsulare – Latin, governing authority that is superior to all other authority.

Makarios – Greek, Strong's ref. 3107. Supremely blessed, by extension, fortunate, well off.

Marc Antony (83 BC – 30 BC) born Marcus Antonius. Roman statesman and military commander. Relative and supporter of Julius Caesar. Carried on a love affair with Cleopatra.

Matsa – Hebrew, Strong's ref. 4672, sufficiently present, to properly come forth.

Matthew Henry – (1662 – 1714) Christian Presbyterian author born in Wales.

Methodeia – Greek, Strong's ref. 3180. Trickery, wile, lie in wait.

Metochos – Greek, Strong's ref. 3353, sharer, partaker.

Optio – Latin, roughly equivalent to modern Lieutenant.

Panteles – Greek, Strong's ref. 3838. Fully ended, entire and complete, uttermost.

Pantote zao – Greek, Strong's ref. 3842, 2198. Ever lives.

Pax Romana – Latin, Roman peace.

Perizonnumi – Greek, Strong's ref. 4024. To gird oneself all around, as in to fasten one's belt.

Phalanx – Greek, a close order military formation of heavy infantry used in the Greek style of ancient combat.

Pilum – Latin, short javelin thought to be designed by Julius Caesar.

Plerophoreo – Greek, Strong's ref. 4135. Completely assured and most assuredly believed to the point of making full proof.

Plutarch – (46 AD - 119 AD) Greek philosopher and historian. Served as priest at the temple of Delphi. Best known for his biographies of famous Greek and Roman figures.

Polybius - (200 BC - 118 BC) Greek historian focusing mostly on Roman history and best known for his work *The Histories*.

Pomerium - Latin, literally - what comes after, or before, the wall. It was used to describe the line demarcating a constituted city and considered a religious boundary.

Pompey the Great - (106 BC - 48 BC) Known as Gnaeus Pompeius Magnus. Roman statesman and military commander. Noted for his skilled military command. Member of the First Triumvirate. Died fighting Julius Caesar on behalf of the Roman Senate.

Poneria - Greek, Strong's ref. 4189, depravity, malice, wickedness.

Praetor - Latin, political appointee for various civil duties, including provincial governorships. Provincial Governors often appointed to overall command of multi-legion armies.

Pugio - Latin, Small knife, dagger. A back-up weapon of the Roman soldier.

Pyrrhus - (319 BC - 272 BC) King of Epirus. Skilled military commander. Considered one of the strongest opponents of the Roman Republic.

Qashab - Hebrew, Strong's ref. 7181, give heed, regard, harken.

Sacramentum - Latin, military oath of allegiance.

Scutum - Latin, large rectangular shaped shield of the type used by Roman soldiers in the 1st century AD.

Skaeva, Cassius - A Roman Centurion in the 1st century BC whom Julius Caesar called out by name in his book, *The Civil Wars*, as courageous in battle.

Sphragizo - Greek, Strong's ref. 4972. To stamp for security or preservation, or seal, seal up.

Sugkleronomos - Greek, Strong's ref. 4789, co-heir, fellow-heir, joint heir.

Sun Tzu - (544 BC - 496 BC) Chinese military commander and writer.

Testudo - Latin, literally tortoise. Term used for a particular Roman infantry formation in which the middle ranks of soldiers hold their shields overhead.

Thlipsis - Greek, Strong's ref. 2347. Pressure, afflicted anguish, burdened persecution, tribulation, trouble.

Thriambeuo - Greek, Strong's ref. 2358. To make an acclamatory procession to commemorate a great victory.

Thureos - Greek, Strong's ref. 2375. Large door shaped shield.

Titus Caesar Vespasianus - (39 AD - 81 AD) Performed military service under the command of his father

Vespasian. Fought in the First Jewish War. Succeeded his father as emperor.

Tomoteros - Greek, Strong's ref. 5114. To cut, but more comprehensively and decisively, by implication, with a single stroke.

Touto - Greek, Strong's ref. 5124, that thing.

Tribunus militum - Latin, roughly equivalent to modern Colonel.

Tsaba - Hebrew, Strong's ref. 6635, mass of people organized for war.

Umbo - Latin, dish-shaped steel plate covering the central handle of a shield.

Varus - (46 BC - 9 AD) born Publius Quinctilius Varus. Famously remembered for having led three legions to destruction by following the turncoat German Arminius into the Teutoberg Forest ambush.

Vegetius - (3rd century AD) born Publius Flavius Renatus Vegetius. Writer of the late Roman Empire. Little is known of the author other than the books he wrote.

Vercingetorix - (80 BC - 46 BC) Chieftain of the Gallic Arverni tribe. United many Gallic tribes in a revolt against Rome which was defeated by Julius Caesar.

Vespasian – (9 AD – 79 AD) Born Titus Flavius Vespasianus. Roman military commander of the famed 10th Legion who later became emperor.

Vir triumphalis – Latin, man of victory, in reference to the recipient and leader of a Roman triumphal parade.

William Magee – (1821 – 1891) Irish reformation preacher. In his various services in the ministry, he was pastor, preacher, bishop, archbishop, treasurer, librarian, curate, dean lecturer and apologist.

Xenophon – (430 BC – 355 BC) Greek military commander and historian from Athens. Led a mercenary army to fight for the Persian Empire. Friend of Socrates.

Yalak – Hebrew, Strong's ref. 3212, to walk, to carry, bring, cause to go on one's way.

YHWH – The name of God in the Hebrew Bible. A tetragrammaton. The English grammatical version with modern vowels is commonly accepted as YaHWeH.

Zao – Greek, Strong's ref. 2198. Living, possessing life.

BIBLIOGRAPHY

Multiple authors, edited by General Sir John Hackett, *Warfare In The Ancient World*. Facts On File, 1989.

Multiple authors, *Caesar's Legions*. Osprey Publishing, 2000.

Multiple authors, *www.biblicalarcheology.org*

Multiple authors, *Fighting Techniques of the Ancient World*. Thomas Dunne Books, St Martin's Press, 2002.

Multiple authors, www.digital.library.villanova.edu

Multiple authors, *The Gospel Coalition*. www.thegospel coalition.org

Multiple authors, Dallas Theological Seminary chapel. www.voice.dts.edu

Anderson, Erich B., *Learning from David and Goliath*. www. warfarehistorynetwork.com, 2015.

Armstrong, John H., *The Coming Evangelical Crisis*. Moody Publishers, 1997.

Beard, Mary, *The Roman Triumph*. Belknap Press of Harvard University, 2007.

Buonaparte, Napoleon, *Military Maxims*. Published 1861 after his death.

Caesar, Julius, *The Gallic Wars*. Commentarii De Bello Gallico. Auto-biographical commentary penned by the famed Roman.

Caesar, Julius, *The Civil Wars*. Commentarii De Bello Civili. Auto-biographical commentary penned by the famed Roman.

Castilo, Jason J., *Endurance And War*. Stanford University Press, 2014.

Chesser, Preston, *The Battle of Actium*. *www.ehistory.osu.edu*

Clausewitz, Carl Von, *Principles of War*. Stackpole Books, 1987.

Constable, Dr. Thomas L., *Notes On Ephesians*. www.planobiblechapel.org. 2024 edition.

Devereaux Brett, *Total Generalship - Collections 2022*. www.acoup.blog

Donaldson, *G.H., In Signaling Communications and the Roman Imperial Army.* Cambridge University Press, 2011.

Dr. Irv Lachow, Mr. David Gompert, Mr. Justin Perkins, *Battle-Wisdom Improving Cognitive Performance in Network Centric Warfare.* Defense Technical Information Center www.apps.dtic.mil 2005

Elliot, Elisabeth, *The Savage My Kinsman.* Vine Books, 1996.

Erickson, Millard J., *Christian Theology.* Baker Book House, 1996.

Featherstone, Donald, *Warriors And Warfare In Ancient And Medieval Times.* Constable and Company Limited, 1997.

Goldsworthy, Adrian, *Roman Warfare.* Cassell & Co., 2000

Goldsworthy, Adrian, *The Punic Wars.* Cassell & Co, 2000

Grant, Michael, *The Twelve Caesars.* Charles Scribner's Sons, 1975.

Haynes Jr, Clarence L., *The Bible Study Club.* www.clarencehaynes.com

Hanson, Victor Davis, *The Wars Of The Ancient Greeks.* Cassell & Company, 2000

Josephus, Flavius (author), Whiston, William, A.M., *The Complete Works*. Thomas Nelson Publishers, 1998.

Kay, Peter, *United Nations of Roma Victrix*. www.unrv.com

Keller, Timothy, *Rediscovering Jonah: The Secret of God's Mercy*. Penguin Books, 2020.

Klein, Christopher, *8 Fascinating Facts About Roman Medicine*. www.history.com 2022.

Leonard, Erin Ph.D, *The Conflict Avoidant: Two Distinct Types*. www.psychologytoday.com 2022

Matyszak, Philip, *Ancient Rome on Five Denarii a Day*. Thames & Hudson, 2007.

Murray, John, *Definitive Sanctification*. Calvin Theological Journal, 1967. *www.monergism.com*

Peterson, Daniel, *The Roman Legions*. The Crowood Press, 1998

Robert Jamieson, Andrew Fausset, and David Brown, *Commentary Critical and Explanitory on the Whole Bible*. Originally published 1871.

Roth, Jonathan, *The Logistics of the Roman Army at War (246 BC - AD 235)*. Brill Academic Publishers, 2012.

Smith, William, *A Dictionary of Greek and Roman Antiquities*. First published by Liitle, Brown and Company, 1859.

Strong, James, LL.D., S.T.D., *The New Strong's Exhaustive Concordance Of The Bible*. Thomas Nelson Publishers, 1990.

Swindoll, Charles R., *So, You Want To Be Like Christ*. Thomas Nelson, 2007.

Vegetius, Publius Flavius Renatus, *De Re Militarii*, Concerning Military Matters. Probably written in the 4th century and possibly revised in the 5th century.

Whitney, Don, *How Can I Be Sure I'm A Christian*. NavPress, 1994

Zodhiates, Spiros, *The Hebrew-Greek Key Study Bible*. AMG Publishers, 1994.

Suggested Reading

Multiple authors, *Rose Book of Bible Charts, Maps & Timelines*. Rose Publishing, 2005.

Duriez, Colin, *AD 33: The Year That Changed The World*. Inter Varsity Press, 2006.

Grant, Michael, *From Alexander To Cleopatra*. Charles Scribner's Sons, 1982.

Grant, Michael, *The Ancient Mediterranean*. Penguin Publishing Group, 1988.

Gonzalez, Justo, *The Story of Christianity*. Prince Press, 1999.

Isserlin, B.S.J., *The Israelites*. Thames and Hudson Ltd, 1998.

Matyszak, Philip, *Chronicle Of The Roman Republic*. Thames & Hudson, 2003.

Tacitus, Publius Cornelius (author), Church, Alfred (translator), *The Annals & The Histories*. Modern Library, 2003.

ABOUT THE AUTHOR

Marty Howes is a living history reenactor. He also is a follower of Christ who believes what Jesus told Nicodemus; "you must be born again to enter the kingdom of heaven."

For 30+ years Marty has held many roles in churches around the world, in full time and layman positions. He has experienced in his life, and witnessed in the lives of others, the constant struggle of God's perfection vs. the corruption of the world.

Marty has spent over four decades studying ancient history. He has participated in several seasons of archaeology field work to include 2 seasons on a Roman site in Wiesbaden Germany. He has also performed experimental archaeology for many years, and even gained access to unpublished data from universities globally. In this role he was featured in the History Channel documentary *Crime And Punishment in the Ancient World*.

His goal is to help others enrich their knowledge of biblical understanding through deeper insight into the historical context of holy scripture.

Printed in the United States
by Baker & Taylor Publisher Services